First World War
and Army of Occupation
War Diary
France, Belgium and Germany

39 DIVISION
Divisional Troops
Gloucestershire Regiment
13th (Service) Battalion (Forest of Dean) (Pioneers)
3 March 1916 - 31 May 1919

WO95/2577/1

The Naval & Military Press Ltd
www.nmarchive.com
Published in association with The National Archives

Published by

The Naval & Military Press Ltd

Unit 10 Ridgewood Industrial Park,

Uckfield, East Sussex,

TN22 5QE England

Tel: +44 (0) 1825 749494

www.naval-military-press.com

www.nmarchive.com

This diary has been reprinted in facsimile from the original. Any imperfections are inevitably reproduced and the quality may fall short of modern type and cartographic standards.

© Crown Copyright
Images reproduced by permission of The National Archives, London, England, 2015.

Contents

Document type	Place/Title	Date From	Date To
Heading	WO95/2577/1		
Heading	13th Bn Gloster Regt (Pioneers) Mar 1916 1919 May		
Miscellaneous	Battalion Disembarked Havre 4.3.16 1/13th Battalion Gloucestershire Regiment (Pioneers) March 1916		
War Diary	Witley Surrey	03/03/1916	03/03/1916
War Diary	Southampton	03/03/1916	03/03/1916
War Diary	Havre	03/03/1916	05/03/1916
War Diary	Thiennes	06/03/1916	06/03/1916
War Diary	Steenbecque	06/03/1916	09/03/1916
War Diary	Estaires	10/03/1916	10/03/1916
War Diary	Laventie	11/03/1916	11/03/1916
War Diary	Belle Rive	26/03/1916	28/03/1916
Heading	Pioneers 39th Division. 1/13th Battalion Gloucestershire Regiment (Pioneers) April 1916		
War Diary	Belle Rive	12/04/1916	12/04/1916
War Diary	Essars	14/04/1916	30/04/1916
Heading	Pioneers 39th Division. 1/13th Battalion Gloucestershire Regiment (Pioneers) May 1916		
War Diary	Essars	01/05/1916	31/05/1916
Map			
Map	Appendix I		
Heading	Pioneers 39th Division. 1/13th Battalion Gloucestershire Regiment (Pioneers) June 1916		
War Diary	Essars	01/06/1916	16/06/1916
War Diary	Lacouture	16/06/1916	30/06/1916
Miscellaneous	Appendix A		
Heading	39th Division. Pioneers 1/13th Battalion Gloucestershire Regiment (Pioneers) July 1916		
Miscellaneous	D.A.G. 3rd Echelon	31/07/1916	31/07/1916
War Diary	Lacouture	01/07/1916	06/07/1916
War Diary	Gorre	07/07/1916	07/07/1916
War Diary	Beuvry Wimpolest	08/07/1916	12/07/1916
War Diary	Wimpole St	13/07/1916	14/07/1916
War Diary	Gorre	15/07/1916	25/07/1916
Miscellaneous	Appendix I		
Miscellaneous			
Miscellaneous	Addendum No. 1	22/06/1916	22/06/1916
Heading	Pioneers 39th Division. 1/13th Battalion Gloucestershire Regiment (Pioneers) August 1916		
War Diary	Gorre	01/08/1916	10/08/1916
War Diary	Lozinghem	10/08/1916	10/08/1916
War Diary	Ostreville	11/08/1916	11/08/1916
War Diary	Le Quesnel	12/08/1916	22/08/1916
War Diary	Rebreuve	23/08/1916	23/08/1916
War Diary	Baudricourt	24/08/1916	24/08/1916
War Diary	Warnimont Wood	25/08/1916	25/08/1916
War Diary	Mailly Maillet Camp	26/08/1916	26/08/1916
War Diary	Mailly Maillet	27/08/1916	31/08/1916
Heading	Pioneers 39th Division. 1/13th Battalion Gloucestershire Regiment (Pioneers) September 1916		

Type	Description	Start	End
War Diary	Mailly Maillet Wood	01/09/1916	03/09/1916
War Diary	Q 27arb	04/09/1916	04/09/1916
War Diary	Mailly Maillet Wood	05/08/1916	07/08/1916
War Diary	Dugouts P 18 Central	07/09/1916	21/09/1916
War Diary	Mailly-Maillet	21/09/1916	30/09/1916
Miscellaneous	Left Half Coy. Operation On Sept 3 Appendix A		
Miscellaneous	Operation September 3rd.	11/09/1916	11/09/1916
Heading	Pioneers 39th Division. 1/13th Battalion Gloucestershire Regiment (Pioneers) October 1916		
War Diary	Mailly Maillet	01/10/1916	03/10/1916
War Diary	Englebelmer	04/10/1916	07/10/1916
War Diary	Pioneer Ra Etc	09/10/1916	31/10/1916
Miscellaneous	C.R.E. 39th Division Appendix A	15/10/1916	15/10/1916
Miscellaneous	I Appendix B		
Heading	Pioneers 39th Division. 1/13th Battalion Gloucestershire Regiment (Pioneers) November 1916		
Miscellaneous	D.A.G. 3rd Echelon. Base.	12/12/1916	12/12/1916
War Diary	Pioneer Road	01/11/1916	15/11/1916
War Diary	Longuevillette	16/11/1916	16/11/1916
War Diary	Autheux	17/11/1916	17/11/1916
War Diary	Poperinghe	18/11/1916	18/11/1916
War Diary	Zeggers Cappel	19/11/1916	20/11/1916
War Diary	Ypres	02/12/1916	25/12/1916
Miscellaneous	Headquarters 39th Division	16/11/1916	16/11/1916
Miscellaneous	Report on Operation	16/11/1916	16/11/1916
Heading	Pioneers 39th Division. 1/13th Battalion Gloucestershire Regiment (Pioneers) December 1916		
War Diary	Ypres	02/12/1916	27/12/1916
Heading	13th Bn Gloster Regt. 1917 Sept To 1919 May From 39 Div Troops		
War Diary	Ypres	01/01/1917	25/04/1917
War Diary	Canal Bank Ypres	01/05/1917	04/08/1917
War Diary	Vlamertinghe	05/08/1916	05/08/1916
War Diary	Berthen	08/08/1916	08/08/1916
War Diary	Vierstraat	15/08/1916	28/09/1916
War Diary	S 2 a 50 Sheet 28 Belgium/France	29/09/1916	29/09/1916
War Diary	Locre	02/10/1917	02/10/1917
War Diary	Vierstraat	16/10/1917	30/10/1917
War Diary	Voormezeele	01/11/1917	16/11/1917
War Diary	Ypres	24/11/1917	26/11/1917
War Diary	Ypres N	01/12/1917	07/12/1917
War Diary	Esche	08/12/1917	08/12/1917
War Diary	Bournonville (Lumbres Area)	10/12/1917	30/12/1917
War Diary	Mention in Dispatches Promotions etc		
War Diary	Casualties Officers Joining		
War Diary	Elverdinghe	01/01/1918	20/01/1918
War Diary	Proven	21/01/1918	21/01/1918
War Diary	Chignolles	26/01/1918	26/01/1918
War Diary	Haut Allaines	30/01/1918	30/01/1918
War Diary	Gauzeaucourt	01/02/1918	28/02/1918
Heading	13th Battn. The Gloucestershire Regiment. March 1918		
War Diary	Gauzeaucourt Sector	01/03/1918	12/03/1918
War Diary	Beaumetz	12/03/1918	30/03/1918
Heading	Pioneers 39th Division. Composite Brigade. Formed part of No. 2 Composite Battalion 11.4.18. 1/13th Battalion Gloucestershire Regiment April 1918		

War Diary		01/04/1918	30/04/1918
Miscellaneous	Special Order Of The Day by Major General C.A. Blacklock C.M.G. D.S.O. Commanding 39th Division Appendix	25/04/1918	25/04/1918
War Diary		05/05/1918	27/07/1918
Heading	War Diary Of 13th Gloucesters From Aug 1st 1918 To 31st Vol No		
War Diary		15/08/1918	24/10/1918
Heading	War Diary Of 13th. Battalion Gloucestershire Regiment From 1st Novr. 1918 To 30th. Novr. 1918		
War Diary		11/11/1918	11/11/1918
War Diary	Haudricourt	04/12/1918	30/12/1918
War Diary	Le Havre	01/01/1919	31/05/1919

W095/25771

39TH DIVISION

13TH BN GLOSTER REGT
(PIONEERS)
MAR 1916 – ~~AUG 1919~~ 1919 MAY

also
for – May 1919

Pioneers 39th Division.

(Forest of Dean)
- - - - -

Battalion disembarked Havre 4. 3. 16.

1/13th BATTALION

GLOUCESTERSHIRE REGIMENT

(Pioneers)

MARCH 1 9 1 6

WAR DIARY or INTELLIGENCE SUMMARY

Army Form C. 2118

Summary of Events and Information of 13th (FOREST OF DEAN) BATT. GLO'STER REGT

Place	Date 1916	Hour	Summary of Events and Information	Remarks and references to Appendices
Witley, Surrey	March 3	5.6.p.m.	Battalion entrained for Southampton.	Volume II
Southampton	" "	7.30 p.m.	Battalion sailed for France. Lt:Col: Boulton and four companies in the "Invicta", Major Lyons Wilson with Transport and details in the "Maidan".	W
Havre	" 4	6.30 a.m.	Battalion arrived at Havre, unloaded the two ships and proceeded to Docks Rest Camp for the night.	W
Havre	" 5	3.98 a.m.	Battalion entrained in two trains, the 1st under Lt Col Boulton, taking the battalion less 150 men & the transport, and 4 officers, who formed the 2nd train, under Major Lyons Wilson. Journey via Rouen, Abbeville, St Omer & Hazebrouck.	W
Thiennes	" 6	6 a.m.	Battalion arrived at Thiennes station, detrained and went into No 3 Camp at Steenbecque.	W
Steenbecque	" 6		In camp at Steenbecque, draining camp, making roads etc.	W
"	" 7			
"	" 8			
"	" 9	10 a.m.	The battalion, less "A" Coy marched to Estaires and billeted there for the night. "A" Coy (Captain W.M. De Paula) went to La Motte, to work under Headquarters 3rd Army Corps, making hurdles, fascines etc. & cutting brushwood.	W
Estaires	" 10	10 a.m.	"C" Coy (Major H.R. Howman) marched to Sailly and went into billets there. B Coy (Capt: H. Jones) and "D" Coy (Capt: S.H. Haden) with Headquarters went into billets at Laventie. "C" Coy was attached for instruction to the Home Counties Field Coy, R.E., "B" Coy, to the 155th Field Coy, R.E., and "D" Coy, to the 225th Field Coy. R.E.	W
Laventie	" 11		From this date "B", "C" and "D" Companies were employed daily under their instructing units in constructing strong points, retaining old trenches, building dug-outs and making breast works in rear of the Front Line.	W

WAR DIARY
INTELLIGENCE SUMMARY
13th (FOREST OF DEAN) BATT. GLO'STER REG.

(Erase heading not required.)

Army Form C. 2118

Place	Date	Hour	Summary of Events and Information	Remarks and references to Appendices
Laventie	March 11 onwards		The area of work allotted to "B" Coy was as follows:- (Reference: Squared Map, "Belgium and Part of France" Sheet 36, Edition 6, 1:40.000). From M.24 central, in rear of trenches which run to N.13.6.44. M.24 central is about the centre of the line held by the 8th Division, to which the Battalion was attached. The troops holding the line were the 23rd Infantry Brigade (2nd Middlesex, 2nd Scottish Rifles, 2nd West Yorks & 2nd Devons. The 14th Wards from the 117th Brigade, 39th Division were attached to the 23rd Brigade for instruction.	
			The area of work allotted to "D" Coy was as follows: (Reference as above) from N.13.6.4.4. to N.14.6.77. The line was held by the 2nd Devons.	W.
			The area of work allotted to "C" Coy: was from N.9.a.5.3. to N.16.d central, including Cellar Farm Avenue, Fern Post and Croix Blanche Post. Tramways were laid by this Company at Fleurbaix. The troops in the line were the Lincolns, Kings Royal Rifles and Berkshires. The G.O.C. Division received a most satisfactory report of the work of the three Companies during their period of instruction from the Officers Commanding the units to which they were attached.	
Belle Rive	" 26		Headquarters, "B", "C", "D" Coys: moved into billets at BELLE RIVE about 5 miles N of BETHUNE.	W.
	" 27		"A" Coy rejoined the battalion, leaving an Officer (Lt Saunders) to carry on work at LAMOTTE.	W.
	" 28		The battalion began the construction of a barbed wire entanglement from GORRE – LE HAMEL – LES CHOQUAUX to the LA BASSÉE Canal. This work was carried out under the direction of the Chief Engineer, XI Corps and was supervised by the Artillery Coy, R.E.	W.

O.C. 13th (FOREST OF DEAN) BATT.
THE GLOUCESTERSHIRE REGIMENT

Pioneers
39th Division.

1/13th BATTALION

GLOUCESTERSHIRE REGIMENT

(Pioneers)

APRIL 1 9 1 6:

WAR DIARY
or
INTELLIGENCE SUMMARY
(Erase heading not required.)

Army Form C. 2118

Summary of Events and Information
18th (FOREST OF DEAN) BATT. GLO'STER REGT

Place	Date	Hour	Summary of Events and Information	Remarks and references to Appendices
Belle Rive	Ap. 12		The wiring was completed. A message to the following effect was sent to the C.O by the G.O.C. 39th Division for publication in battalion orders. "Please inform all ranks in 13th Gloucesters that the G.O.C. X1th Corps is highly satisfied with the excellent work done by your battalion on the wiring on the 3rd line. He thinks it an excellent job and thoroughly well carried out. I am very pleased and gratified with the excellent report."	Volume III ws
"	Ap. 7		"A" Coy moved to Beuvry to work on the 3rd Line defences at Cambrin. They were attached to the 18th Bn Middlesex Regt.	ws
ESSARS	Ap. 14		The Battalion took over from the 19th Battalion WELCH Regt. (Pioneers) of the 38th Division. Head quarters and all companies were billeted in ESSARS. The 39th Division at this time took over their part of the line. The work of the 13th Glosters was draining, making and renewing trenches in rear of the line FESTUBERT – GIVENCHY – LA BASSEE CANAL. Also connecting up the "Islands" on the same line.	ws
	Ap. 23		The party left at LAMOTTE under Lieut SAUNDERS joined at ESSARS. A most complimentary report of their work was forwarded to the 39th Division by the O.C. FOREST CONTROL, 1st ARMY.	ws
	Ap. 26	7.30 a.m. 9.30 a.m.	2nd Lt Callaway joined vice Lt HILLIER, wounded. Asphyxiating and weeping gas were experienced at ESSARS, but only to a slight extent. No casualties.	ws
	Ap. 28	11 p.m.	Night working parties were exposed to gas, without casualties.	ws
	Ap. 30		Casualties were very slight up to the end of this month, only 1 Officer (Lt G.S.Z. HILLIER) and three other ranks being wounded, none seriously except the Officer.	ws

Alf. Whitten Lt Col
O.C. 13th (F. of D.) BATT.
THE GLOUCESTERSHIRE REGIMENT

Pioneers.
39th Division.

1/13th BATTALION

GLOUCESTERSHIRE REGIMENT   (Pioneers)

M A Y 1 9 1 6

WAR DIARY
or
INTELLIGENCE SUMMARY

(Erase heading not required.)

Army Form C. 2118

Summary of Events and Information
13th (FOREST OF DEAN) BATT. GLO'STER REGT.

Place	Date	Hour	Summary of Events and Information	Remarks and references to Appendices
ESSARS	MAY 1.		Work continued as last month.	
			A. Coy continued to reclaim PIONEER ROAD.	
			D Coy worked on the back end of FIFE RD, GEORGE ST, and LOOP ROAD from GEORGE ST to the ISLANDS. Also on BARNTON ROAD from the OLD GERMAN LINE to the ISLANDS and on the old Breastwork between.	2.9 WW See Appendix 1
			C Coy worked on OXFORD TERRACE, CAMBRIDGE TERRACE, GLASGOW ST, BAYSWATER and the upper (east) end of ORCHARD ROAD. Also on CHEYNE WALK and the WILLOW.	L.MN See Appendix 2
			B Coy worked on the drainage system of the Divisional Area, and a portion of the 35th Divisional Area. The main Drains ran through a portion of the latter area and extended in the vicinity of INDIAN VILLAGE, FESTUBERT (Appendix 2) GIVENCHY & So to the LA BASSEE CANAL. (Appendix 3)	MWL.
	MAY 28.	3 p.m.	Orders received to evacuate half ESSARS for the reception of the 118 Brigade, who marched in during the night 28/29 MAY. On this night the Divisional Infantry handed over the FESTUBERT section of the line and took over the AUCHY section, immediately S. of the LA BASSEE CANAL.	LMW

Army Form C. 2118

WAR DIARY
or
INTELLIGENCE SUMMARY

(Erase heading not required.)

Summary of Events and Information
13th (FOREST OF DEAN) BATT. GLO'STER REGT.

Place	Date	Hour	Summary of Events and Information	Remarks and references to Appendices
ESSARS	May 31		Casualties during the month were as follows – Officers: Killed None. Wounded One (2Lt CROCK-FORD) Slightly. OTHER RANKS - Killed: One. Died of Wounds: Two. Wounded: Thirteen. Accidentally Wounded: Two. During the month the following Officers joined the Battalion: 2Lt F.H. LA TROBE, 2Lt J.G. PAULING and 2Lt A.O. MILES. A draft of 20 O.R. arrived on the 20th and one of 3 O.R. on the 29th. Lt W.T. BROWN R.A.M.C. relieved Lt ANGUS CAMPBELL on 28th Ineny. Lt CAMPBELL was transferred to the MINING RESCUE SCHOOL at BETHUNE.	2ADTS. 2ADTS. 2ADTS.
ESSARS	31.5.16.			

J.F. Wynne Willson
Major
for Lt. Col:
Commanding 13th GLOSTERS.

Appendix B.2

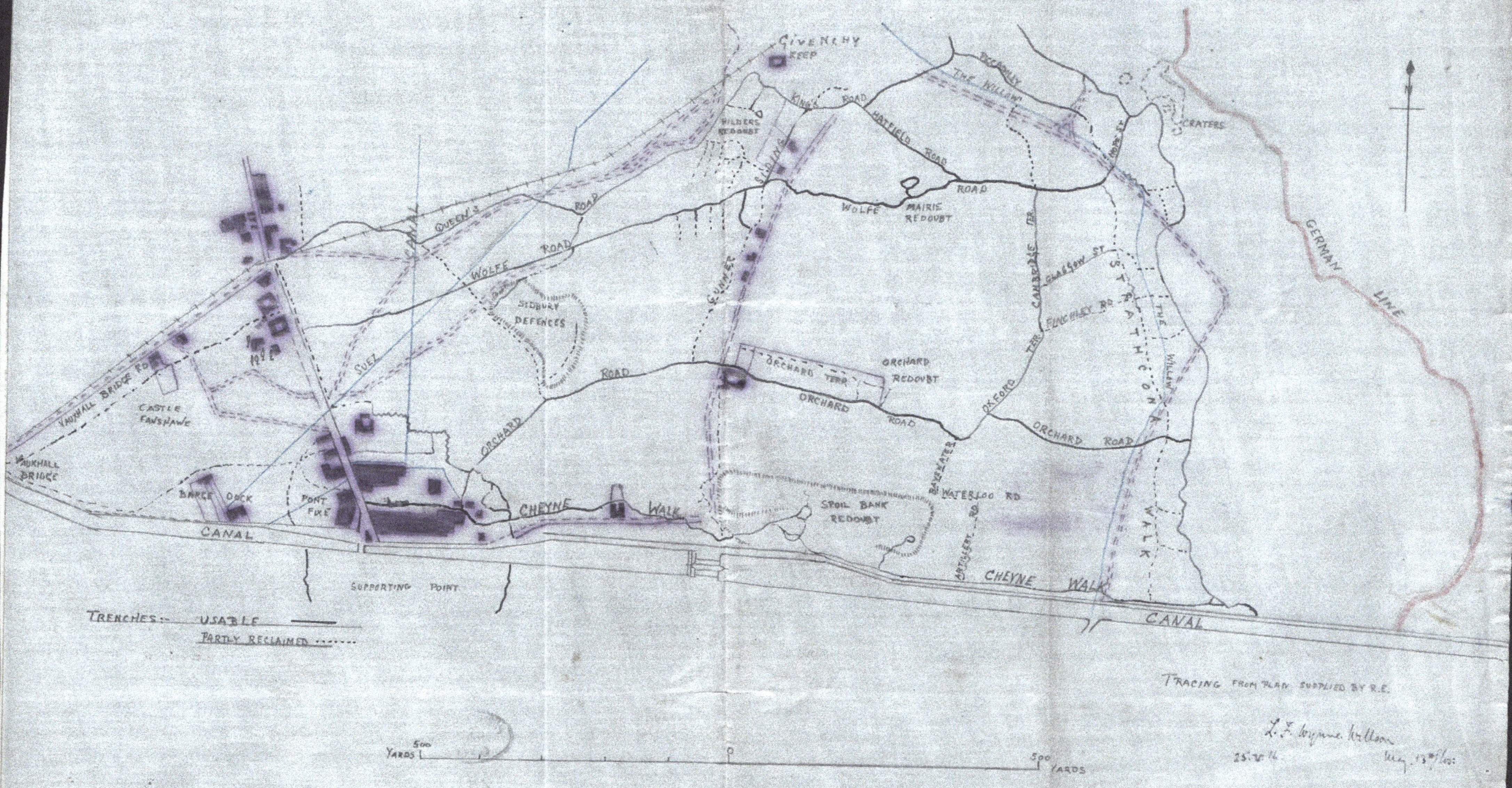

TRACING FROM PLAN SUPPLIED BY R.E.

25.V.16

APPENDIX I.

Indian Village

la Quinque Rue

Brewery Corner
Rue de Cailloux

Festubert

le Plantin

Willow Road

Yellow Road

Tracing of Brigade Trench Map AREA "G" Edition A December 1915. Portions of 36 SW 3 & 36 NW 1.

Scale 1:10,000

Work referred to in DIARY outlined in green
Trenches

Pioneers
39th Division.

1/13th BATTALION

GLOUCESTERSHIRE REGIMENT

(Pioneers)

J U N E 1 9 1 6 ::

June
13. Gloucester
Army Form C. 2118
Vol 4

3.N.
63 sheets

WAR DIARY.
or
INTELLIGENCE SUMMARY.
(Erase heading not required.)

39 XXXIX

Summary of Events and Information
13th (FOREST OF DEAN) BATT. GLO'STER REGT.

Place	Date 1916	Hour	Summary of Events and Information	Remarks and references to Appendices
ESSARS	June 1		Work continued by all companies as last month.	
LACOUTURE	June 16		Battalion moved into billets at LACOUTURE. The 39th Division took over the FERME DU BOIS section of the line, handing over the GIVENCHY section to the 33rd Division on our right. The 61st Division was on our left.	LAHTI
			"A" Coy: continued to work on PIONEER ROAD.	
			"B" " " " " SUEZ CANAL and also on the COURANT DE BREUVE.	
			"C" " " took over repairs to ROPE WALK and PIPE ST.	
			"D" " " continued work on the ISLANDS and completed the BREASTWORK mentioned last month.	
"	June 25 3-4.30pm		LACOUTURE bombarded by 4.2 Field Howitzers. Two direct hits on B Coy's transport billets. 4 men wounded.	amours
"	June 25		A party consisting of 9 Officers and 285 men with a proportion of N.C.O's moved to PACAUT to practise pioneer work in connection with a proposed trench attack. CAPT. H.D. HILLIER was in command of the party, which was under the orders of the G.O.C. 116 Brigade.	
"	June 29/30 3.20 am		The trench attack mentioned above took place on the night 29/30. The objective was the German first and second line on either side of THE BOAR'S HEAD, from S.10.d.0.2 to S.16.a 7.2. The battalion furnished parties to dig communication trenches in rear of the assaulting infantry. A coy: with 50 men, connecting Sap at S.16.a 7.2. C coy extending BOND ST, B Coy: extending VINE ST + D Coy making a breast work at S.10.d.0.2. The infantry were the 116 Bde, consisting of 11th, 12th + 13th Sussex and 14th Hants with detachments of R.E.	

REFERENCE France Bethune contoured Serve des Bois + Estaliques Section 1/10000 Revised Edition

Army Form C. 2118

WAR DIARY
or
INTELLIGENCE SUMMARY
(Erase heading not required.)

Summary of Events and Information
13th (FOREST OF DEAN) BATT. GLO'STER REGT.

Instructions regarding War Diaries and Intelligence Summaries are contained in F. S. Regs., Part II. and the Staff Manual respectively. Title Pages will be prepared in manuscript.

Place	Date	Hour	Summary of Events and Information	Remarks and references to Appendices
LACOUTURE	June 30		A short report with approximate casualties is attached as appendix A A full report will be furnished with the diary of the month of July. Officers killed. 2Lt A.O. Miles Officers wnd: Lt R.P. Wild, 2Lt N.H. Langley Smith, 2Lt L.K. Collins	A.
		30.6.16	J.J. Wynne William Major to O.C. 13th Glosters.	

1875 Wt. W593/826 1,000,000 4/15 J.B.C. & A. A.D.S.S./Forms/C. 2118.

Appendix A.

"A"

This party reached starting point ten minutes before time and was organized into carrying parties to carry up their pickets and hurdles which I had dumped near entrance to CADBURYS C.T. Carrying commenced at 12.5 a.m.

Owing to failure of pipe pusher mine breastwork could not be constructed, so a trench was dug, but could not reach enemy saps at BOARS HEAD owing to devil enemy wire, which was not cut.

Work was made almost impossible from the beginning by parties of R.E. trying to get through the saps with hurdles, etc., while the infantry were already using it to retire through.

Party was then utilised to man fire trenches, as a counter-attack was expected. There were not enough Infantry to do this.

At 6.15 a.m. after consultation with the Infantry Officer i/c of that part of the line the Pioneers were withdrawn, leaving two Lewis Guns and team under M. G. Sergeant.

Approximate casualties: 1 Officer.
                         10 O.R.

"B"

This party arrived at starting point two minutes before time and followed their route to position.

At 3.12 a.m. this party went over into No Man's Land, laid out Communication Trench with Cord and Electric Torch held by an N.C.O. in the German Communication Trench, our trench was to join up with.

Germans were holding their front line two bays Northward from where we joined it.

This party succeeded in completing this Communication Trench in spite of losing both its officers. Depth of digging taken out varied from 2' to 5' and gave good cover all the way.

This Communication Trench was used for Ammunition Supply.

At times the men had to stop digging to drive off hostile bombing parties approaching from the left flank.

This party was withdrawn about 6 a.m.

    Casualties: 2 Officers.
           42 O.R.

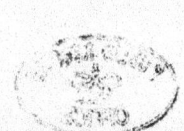

"C".

This party arrived at position of assembly at 1.10 a.m. and proceeded by route to position, which owing to obstruction was not reached till 3.20 a.m.

At this time what was thought to be the third wave of Infantry was retiring, and under these circumstances the officer i/c decided that work on the proposed Communication T. was not possible.

He then reported to nearest Infantry Commander who ordered him to man the empty fire bays in front line between Vine and Bond Street, and this was done.

Later he was ordered to clear two Communication Trenches, Vine and Bond Streets (which had been blown in) to enable wounded to be evacuated.

On completion of this work he received permission from Officer i/c Infantry to withdraw his men.

Casualties: 1 Officer.
16 O.R.

D.

This party reached starting point eight minutes before time and followed route to position.

On arrival at position a lot of Infantry were still there and the Officer i/c was informed that this was the fourth wave which had not yet gone over.

Pioneers stood by in bays off HAZARA and the officers in charge of party went forward to front line and found remnants of our third wave coming back under heavy shelling and M.G.fire.

The front German line where the left flank breastwork was to join it was never taken by our infantry.

Under these circumstances work was impossible.

This party then was moved up into front line to man empty fire bays on an order being received from the right that this was to be done. Two Lewis Guns with this party were also placed in position here.

There being no Infantry Officers to report to in this part of the line, the Officer i/c of this party organized his men and any Infantry who came under his control.

On receipt of a verbal message that ammunition was urgently required by our troops holding the German line to the right he organized an ammunition party and proceeded with it up "B" Party's continuation of COPSE STREET and delivered two boxes to the Infantry who had sent for it.

He attempted to get up a third box and some Mills Grenades but owing to the intensity of the fire on our breastwork, was unable to again cross it.

This party later went over again and brought in several wounded.

The party was finally withdrawn on receipt of my orders between 7 a.m. and 8 a.m.. Some Infantry who had then come into this part of the line taking over the fire bays.

        Officers: Nil.   O.R. 8.

39th Division.
Pioneers

1/13th BATTALION

GLOUCESTERSHIRE REGIMENT

(pioneers)

JULY 1916

39. L.P. 663.

D.A.G.
   3rd Echelon

vol 5

Herewith War Diary of this battalion for the month of July.

H Brodie Capt. & Adj
for LT. COL.
O.C. 13th (FOREST OF DEAN) BATT.
THE GLOUCESTERSHIRE REGIMENT.

31.7.16.

Should be sent through Div HQ

Yes

Yes

H.N.

Army Form C. 2118

WAR DIARY
or
INTELLIGENCE SUMMARY
(Erase heading not required.)

Summary of Events and Information
13th (FOREST OF DEAN) BATT. GLO'STER REGT.

Place	Date	Hour	Summary of Events and Information	Remarks and references to Appendices
LACOUTURE	July 1.	6—	Summary [illegible] of "B" Coy [illegible]	
			Quiet day. Usual working parties at night. 2 Vowels with one Sergt. went out to try	
		10 p.m.	to recover wounded reported still alive in NO MAN'S LAND. Unsuccessful. Heavy bombardment of Divisions on our right and left.	LOWW.
	July 3	9.45 a.m.	The raiding party paraded before General Hacking, Comdg. XI th Corps and were complimented on their work.	WWW WWW.
		9.30 p.m.	Raid by 117 Bde in FESTUBERT sect on. No working parties sent up.	
"	July 6	9.30 p.m.	Battalion, less B Coy, moved to GORRE. "B" Coy remained in LACOUTURE.	
GORRE	" 7	9.15 p.m.	Battalion left GORRE for the line. Took over keeps and VILLAGE LINE in AUCHY section from 4th SUFFOLKS. Relief completed at midnight.	
		11 p.m.	LACOUTURE bombarded.	
	" 8	3 p.m.	"C" Company taken from keeps to take over mining work at AUCHY section. Headquarters moved to BEUVRY. Transport + C Coy billeted there. Major WYNNE WILLSON with A + D Coys left in line, HQ at WIMPOLE ST	
BEUVRY WIMPOLE ST	" 9	11 a.m.	Men from VILLAGE LINE put into Keeps	
		8.30 p.m.	Left keeps and took over VILLAGE LINE and FACTORY TRENCH. Handed over to 12st R. Sussex "B" Company moved to GORRE.	
	" 10		Working, carrying and mining working parties furnished to 116 Bde and 251 Tunnelling Coy R.E.	
	" 11		MAISON ROUGE heavily bombarded at 4 p.m. 10th working party under 2 Lt LATROBE engaged in	
	" 12		support of infantry (13th R. Sussex) in repelling German raid near No 11 Bricks tack. Successful. No casualties.	

Army Form C. 2118

WAR DIARY
or
INTELLIGENCE SUMMARY
(Erase heading not required.)

Summary of Events and Information
13th (FOREST OF DEAN) BATT. GLO'STER REGT.

Place	Date	Hour	Summary of Events and Information	Remarks and references to Appendices
WIMPOLE ST.	July 13	6 pm	Parties as usual.	AAAAS
"	July 14	9.30 p	Headquarters & "C" Company moved to GORRE.	AAAAS
GORRE	" 15	9.30 p	Stores in VILLAGE LINE and FACTORY TREVEN handed over to 22nd DURHAM Lt INFANTRY, 8th DIV. Pioneers.	AAAAS
"	"	3.30 am	Detachment from line moved to GORRE.	AAAAS
GORRE	" 16		Battalion in Divisional reserve, ready to move at an hours notice	AAAAS
"	" 21		Each Company attached to a Field Coy. R.E. for work. A to No 234 Coy. Area of work. GIVENCHY R & LaCouture.	AAAAS
			B Drainage.	
			C " No 227 "	FERME DU BOIS.
			D " No 225 "	FESTUBERT (COVERTRENCH)
				AAAAS
"	" 24th		C Company moved to LACOUTURE	AAAAS
			Battalion concentrated at GORRE. C Company returned from LACOUTURE.	AAAAS
			2 Lieut A.L. CROCKFORD awarded military cross } for conspicuous bravery in action of night	
			19494 Sgt. R.A. TRESISE } Distinguished Conduct Medal } June 29/30. D.R.O. No 306. 24.7.16	
			18177 Pte T.G. BOLTON }	AAAAS
			18149 Sgt H.T. Sutton } Military medal.	AAAAS
			19831 Cpl R.W. Snelles }	
			The following Officers joined the Battalion 2 Lieuts. S.T. FELSTEAD, H. STARKIE, R.A. DRAKE, C.W.J. JERVIS, E.C. HALSON, W.A. KING, A.C. BAKER, E.R.V. COLLETT, W.J. BRADLEY.	AAAAS
	25th		Under a new scheme of work, the Companies were employed in the following keeps and trenches	
			A. Coy. GUNNER SIBING, PICCADILLY, OXFORD & CAMBRIDGE TERRACE. D. Coy. COVER TRENCH, CANADIAN ORCHARD.	AAAAS
			C. " LOOP ROAD, EPINETTE EAST KEEP, FESTUBERT CENTRAL KEEP. LOOP ROAD	
			B Coy continued on drainage work	

Army Form C. 2118

WAR DIARY

INTELLIGENCE SUMMARY

(Erase heading not required.)

Summary of Events and Information
13th (FOREST OF DEAN) BATT. GLO'STER REGT.

Place	Date	Hour	Summary of Events and Information	Remarks and references to Appendices
GORRE			Report on Operations at BOAR'S HEAD on night of June 29/30 attached as Appendix I. Map references to Secret French map. Casualties of the month. — Other ranks killed 2, died of wounds 1, wounded 12.	I attd.
			In the attack on BOAR'S HEAD, June 30. —	
			Officers. O.R.	
			Killed 1 10	
			Died of wounds — 1	
			Wounded 4 57	
			Missing — 13	
	31/7/16.		J F Wynne Wilson Major for O C 13th/15th Gloucestershire Regt.	

APPENDIX I

Notes on attack on German Front Line, North of the BOAR'S HEAD. Night June 29/30, 1916.

For the above, 285 men, with a proportion of Officers and N.C.O's, were attached to the 116th Infantry Brigade, which was the Brigade selected for the work.

MAIN INTENTION.   To capture and hold enemy front trench from S.16.a.40.6. to S.10.d.17.45. and The support trench from S.16.a.65.55. to S.10.d.25.20. connecting the captured position to our present line on the left and right flanks at S.16.a.3.3. and S.10.d.08.62. respectively.

PIONEER PLAN.

See Sketch Map.   The pioneers were organized in four parties, representative of the four Companies, and in future styled "A", "B", "C", or "D", in accordance with the Company from which they were drawn.

From right to left.   "A"   To connect FISHTAIL SAP with German Sap running out from BOARS HEAD, by a breast work. In this they were to be assisted by a detachment from No.3. Australian Mining Company, who were to co-operate by blowing a mine by means of the Pipe Forcing Jack between our and the enemy sap.

"C"   To form communication trench to captured position, in continuation of BOND ST.

"B"   To form communication trench to captured position in continuation of COPSE ST.

"D"   To connect our front line and the captured trench by a breastwork.

COLLECTION of MATERIAL.   Owing to the operation having to take place at an earlier date than was expected no material had been collected in forward pioneer dumps, and permission to use R.E. Dumps in front line was obtained.

ASSEMBLY ORDERS.   As per attached table. "A".

REPORT OF WORK OF EACH PARTY.

"A"   This party got a certain number of hurdles etc. up to the point of assembly on the night of the operation. The party waited till 3.10 a.m. and though under heavy shell fire, had no casualties.
At about 3.5. a.m. the Officer in charge of the Pipe Forcing Jack mine reported that he had exploded his mine, and was sorry that it was a failure, a crater having been formed instead of a trench.
At 3.10 an Officer and 8 men went up the sap and found a large crater only a few yards from the end of our sap..They crossed No Man's Land to the end of the German Sap and found the wire was very thick and not destroyed. Men were at once set to join up the saps, working from both ends.

The work was made impossible almost from the beginning by parties of R.E. trying to get through with hurdles while the Infantry were already trying to come back through the partly formed trench. A shallow trench was formed as far as the German wire. The party was ultimately withdrawn on finding that the Infantry had retired and they were working with only Germans in front of them.
They then manned the fire bays in our front line, and reported to officer in charge of infantry who gave them instructions to withdraw about 6.15 a.m.

"C" Here the 4th wave of infantry never went over, and at 3.10 a.m. the third wave was retiring, making it useless for the pioneers to start their work.

"B" Went out at 3.10. A Sergeant and one man went across and sat on German parapet directing the line for the trench with an electric torch. The trench was completed to a maximum depth of 5' and a minimum 2'.

"D" On looking over the parapet at 3.10 the remnants of the third infantry wave coming back under heavy shelling and Machine Gun fire. They were also being bombed from the German front line. Under these circumstances the work was out of question, and the officer in charge of the party reported to the Infantry Commander and manned portions of our front line till ordered to get his party out of the line between 7 and 8 a.m

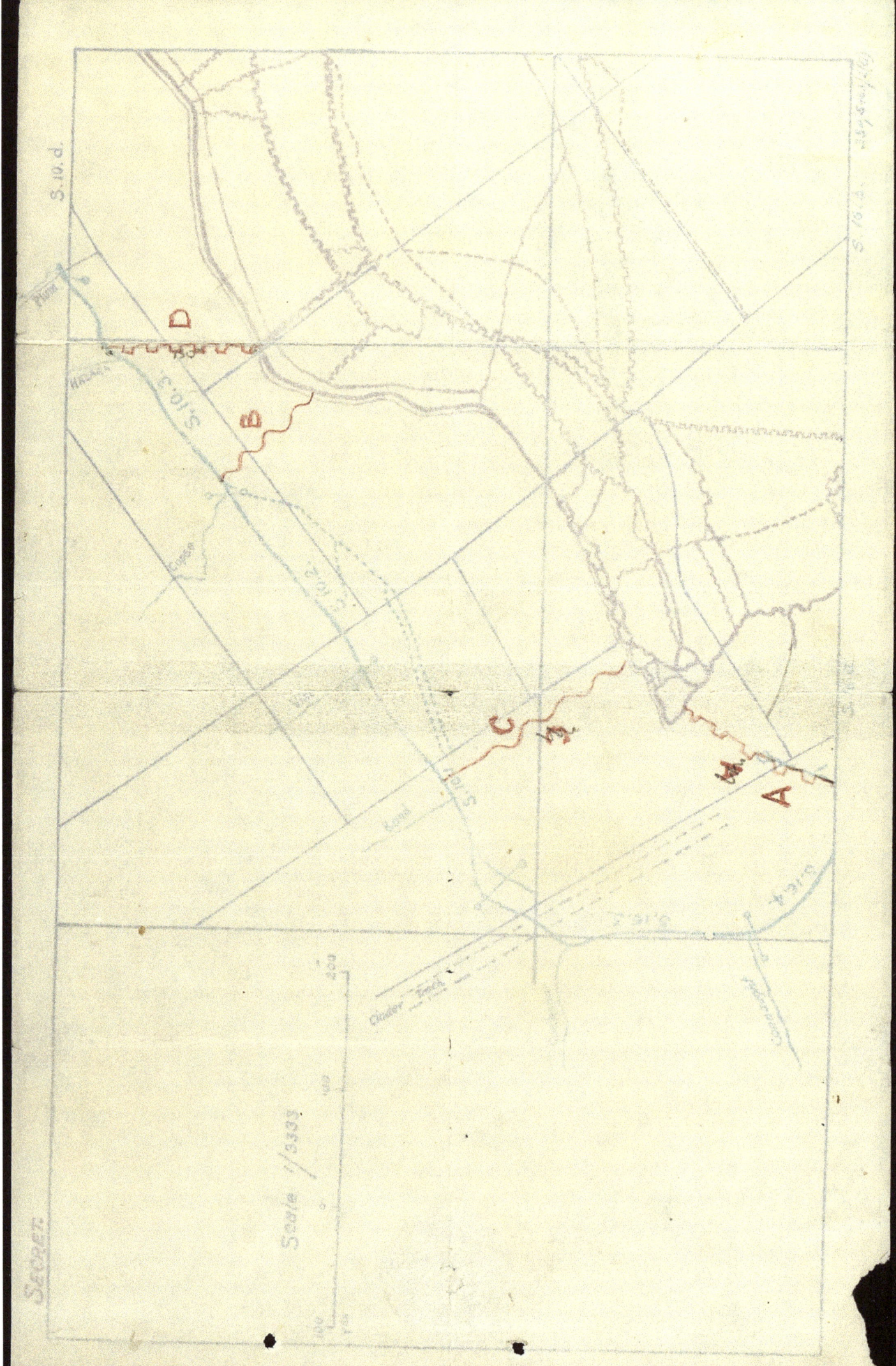

SECRET.   A

                                H.O.4.
           ADDENDUM No. 1.   dated 22.6.1916.
                                 O.7.

   The following are the arrangements for the assembly of the Strong Point
Construction parties, of the Pioneer Parties for the construction of
Breastworks and Communication Trenches, and of Carrying parties for R.E.
material:-

No.	Party Strength.	Task for which intended.	Starting Point.	Route.	Position of assembly.	Time to be ready at position of assembly.	Route from position of assembly to TASK position and time of moving forward.
2.	Pioneers 60. **A**	Right flank breastwork Party.	Road Junction at S.15.a.1.3. on Rue de Bois at 1 hour before zero.	CADBURY'S.	Front trench from FISHTAIL TO CADBURYS.	zero.	To move forward at 2 hours 5 min after zero via FISHTAIL S.P. after No.1. = 3.10 a.m
4.	Pioneers 100. **C**	Bond St. Extension Communication trench.	To arrive junction VINE ST. & RUE DE BOIS & 30 min. before zero.	VINE STREET.	GUARDS RESERVE TRENCH between VINE ST. & BOND ST.	zero.	To move forward two hours 5 min. after zero. = 3.10 a.m
5.	Pioneers 75. **B**	COPSE STREET. extension communication trench.	To arrive junction of COPSE ST. & RUE DE BOIS 45 min. before zero.	COPSE ST.	GUARDS RESERVE. between VINE ST. and COPSE ST.	zero.	To move forward 2 hours 5 minutes after zero. = 3.10 a.m
9.	Pioneers 50. **D**	Left flank breastwork.	To arrive junction of COPSE ST. & RUE DU BOIS 30 mins. before zero.	COPSE ST.	GUARDS RESERVE TRENCH between COPSE ST. and HAZARA STREET.	zero.	To move forward two hours five minutes after zero. = 3.10 a.m

ZERO = 1-5 a.m
night 29/30

Pioneers
39th Division.

1/13th BATTALION

GLOUCESTERSHIRE REGIMENT

(Pioneers)

AUGUST 1 9 1 6

Army Form C. 2118

WAR DIARY
or
INTELLIGENCE SUMMARY
(Erase heading not required.)

Vol 6

Instructions regarding War Diaries and Intelligence Summaries are contained in F.S. Regs., Part II. and the Staff Manual respectively. Title Pages will be prepared in manuscript.

Summary of Events and Information
13th (FOREST OF DEAN) BATT. GLO'STER REGT.

5.N. 2 shut

Place	Date	Hour	Summary of Events and Information	Remarks and references to Appendices
GORRE	August 1		Work as last month for all companies	2/8/915
	5		B + C Companies moved to LE HAMEL, taking over billets of 254 Tunnelling Coy; R.E. Major WYNNE Willson in command of detachment.	6/8/15
	10.	11 a.m.	Battalion relieved by 11th Bn S. LANCS; REGT. (Pioneers, 30th Division).	9/8/15
		5 p.m.	Battalion marched to LOZING HEM and billetted the night there. Horsbrook S.A. 1/100000. F.G. Sequeville 1/20000	10/8/15
LOZINGHEM			2Lt J.L. BERRY 4/5th Black Watch joined the battalion pending transfer.	
OSTREVILLE	11th	4.45 p.m.	Battalion marched to OSTREVILLE and billetted the night there. (LENS 11. 1/100000) E 2. ENV of St POL.	11/8/15
LE QUESNEL	12th	6 p.m.	Battalion marched to LE QUESNEL and billets. All but 12 officers to AVERDOINGT (do.) F.2. Southern half.	12/8/15 12/8/15
	13th	8 a.m.	Two men per Coy. employed on making rifle range near MONCHY LE BRETON F.2. Northern half	
"	14th		do. do.	
"	15th to 20th		Battalion employed digging system of trenches exact replica of a portion of the German and British line. Flammenwerfer demonstration on 20th.	15/8/15
	21st		Rest day	
	22nd		Battalion on musketry at AVERDOINGT	
REBREUVE	23rd		Battalion marched to REBREUVE and billeted there. Under command of G.O.C. 116 Brigade.	
BAUDRICOURT	24th		" " BAUDRICOURT.	
WARNIMONT WOOD	25th		" " WARNIMONT WOOD + bivouaced. On conclusion of march, left 116 Bde.	
MAILLY MAILLET Camp	26th		" " MAILLY MAILLET CAMP, huts + tents.	

WAR DIARY

INTELLIGENCE SUMMARY

Summary of Events and Information
13th (FOREST OF DEAN) BATT. GLO'STER REGT.

Place	Date	Hour	Summary of Events and Information	Remarks and references to Appendices
MAILLY MAILLET	27th		Rest	
	28th		Companies at work A Coy: THIEPVAL WOOD, building emplacements for 3rd M.M.G. Coy.	
			B " CHARLES AVENUE widening and duck boarding New Trench, PROSPECT PT - PETTAGE TRENCH	
			C " CHARLES AVENUE, widening and duck boarding. POINT ST.	
			Camp cleaning.	
			D " New Trench Prospect Point - Pottage Trench	
			LEWIS GUNNERS - widening and duckboarding ROYAL AVENUE	
	29th		Work as usual.	
			" " Camp and vicinity bombarded at 3, 4.15 & 9.15 p.m.	
	30th		" " Camp and vicinity bombarded intermittently from 2 a.m. LEWIS GUNNERS only to work on	
	31st		line. Remainder making Shelter Trench at bottom of Camp.	
			Casualties for the month O.R. 3 Killed	
			O.R. 8 Wounded	

Reference Sheet Trench Map, Sert Mar Q.59.

L/ Col Janes Willson Major
for Lt Col
13th Bn Gloucestershire Regt

Army Form C. 2118

Pioneers
39th Division.

1/13th BATTALION

GLOUCESTERSHIRE REGIMENT

(Pioneers)

SEPTEMBER 1 9 1 6

WAR DIARY
or
~~INTELLIGENCE SUMMARY~~
(Erase heading not required.)

Army Form C. 2118

Vol 7

Instructions regarding War Diaries and Intelligence Summaries are contained in F.S. Regs., Part II. and the Staff Manual respectively. Title Pages will be prepared in manuscript.

Place	Date	Hour	Summary of Events and Information	Remarks and references to Appendices
MAILLY MAILLET WOOD	Sept 1	2 a.m.	Camp heavily bombarded. During day, battalion dug trenches under bank below road, for shelter.	MMW
	2		Continuous bombardment of enemy's line, in preparation for attack tomorrow.	MMW
		4:30 p	Half of "C" Coy under Major Thomann went up to take up position for attack.	
		7:30 "	" " " " " " Capt Davis " " " " " " "	
			(Report of "C" Coy's action attached as appendix "A")	
	3	5 a.m.	Intense bombardment of enemy line started. Attack on enemy trenches began. weather fine. Visibility good. Battalion in Divisional Reserve.	MMW
		6 pm	A, B, & D Coys went up to clean our trenches when blocked by shell fire and corpses. All Companies subjected to 5 hour bombardment with gas shells and H.E. little work possible.	
Q 27 a & b	4		Battalion formed reserve to 118 Bde. Moved up to Reserve Trenches at Q 27 a & b. (Reference Trench Map, France, 57 d S.E, Edition 2 D, 1/20000)	MMW
MAILLY MAILLET WOOD	5	7 pm	Ceased to be attached to 118 Bde. Returned to MAILLY MAILLET WOOD shelters. Wood heavily shelled during night.	MMW
			Dug outs constructed under road below wood.	G.N. 9 sheets MMW

WAR DIARY

Army Form C. 2118

Instructions regarding War Diaries and Intelligence Summaries are contained in F.S. Regs., Part II. and the Staff Manual respectively. Title Pages will be prepared in manuscript.

Place	Date	Hour	Summary of Events and Information	Remarks and references to Appendices
DUG-OUTS P.18 Central	7th		Ordinary Pioneer work. A Coy. making dug-outs in ST JEAN STREET & VICTORIA STREET.	M.M.W.
	8a		B " improving & trench boarding CHARLES AVENUE, ROYAL AVENUE, JACOB'S LADDER.	
			D " " " " GABION AVENUE & CONSTITUTION HILL	M.M.W.
	9a	6-7pm	C " making T.M. emplacements in CONSTITUTION HILL, under 2nd R.A. R.E.	
			Small gas balloons sent over by German, which dropped pamphlets at intervals.	M.M.W.
	10th		No shelling of camp on 8th, 9th or 10th.	M.M.W.
	11th		D Coy. began work on new communication trench along railway embankment in valley of ANCRE. (IRON ROAD)	
	11th ↓ 21st		Work continued as above. On 17th D Coy (1 platoon) employed cleaning & repairing road from Q.28.c.5.7 to Q.28.c.6.3. in MESNIL	
MAILLY – MAILLET	21st	5pm	Battalion moved into billets in MAILLY-MAILLET.	M.M.W.
	24th		Work of B & D Coys. attached to B Coy. improving & trench boarding CHARLES and GABION AVENUES	M.M.W.
			D " " " " TIPPERARY AVENUE. & road in MESNIL	
	25th		No working parties at night.	M.M.W.
	26th		Battalion in reserve to 116 & 118 Brigades. No working parties. "Stood by" from 7.a.m. Zero hour for feint attack by 39th Div. 12.55 p.m.	M.M.W.
	27	midnight	4 Offrs:, 200 O.R. employed as carrying party for 118 Bde.	M.M.W.
		3.30pm	"Stand by" cancelled. Ordinary working parties resumed, except A & D Coys (less MESNIL ROAD party) who were at disposal of 118 Bde. for carrying.	M.M.W.

Army Form C. 2118

WAR DIARY
or
INTELLIGENCE SUMMARY
(Erase heading not required.)

Instructions regarding War Diaries and Intelligence Summaries are contained in F. S. Regs., Part II. and the Staff Manual respectively. Title Pages will be prepared in manuscript.

Place	Date	Hour	Summary of Events and Information	Remarks and references to Appendices
MAILLY-MAILLET	27th	8 p.m. 10 p.m.	Carrying parties for 118 Bde	
"	28th		Ordinary Pioneer work and carrying parties	
	29th 30th		"	
		21st	The following officers left the battalion on transfer – Capt. S.H. Haden to 1/5th GLOUCESTERS	
		27th	2 Lt W A King } S. T. Jelahed } E. C. L. Callaway } to 1st GLOUCESTERS E. R. V. Collett } W. J. Bradley }	
		10th	2 Lt A. G. Kirk to R.F.C.	
		20th 26th	The following officers arrived 2 Lt J. R. Frampton J. V. Taylor	

1875 Wt. W593/826 1,000,000 4/15 J.B.C. & A. A.D.S.S./Forms/C. 2118.

Army Form C. 2118

WAR DIARY
or
INTELLIGENCE SUMMARY

(Erase heading not required.)

Instructions regarding War Diaries and Intelligence Summaries are contained in F. S. Regs., Part II. and the Staff Manual respectively. Title Pages will be prepared in manuscript.

Place	Date	Hour	Summary of Events and Information	Remarks and references to Appendices
MAILLY MAILLET	Sept. 1916		Casualty Report for month	J.M.W.
			Officers O.R.	
			Killed 3	
			Wounded 31	
			Missing 1 (2Lt Bennett) 3	
			Gassed 1 (Lt Stokes) 5	
			Died of Wounds 2	
	30.9.16.			J.A. Wynne Willson Maj. for O.C. 13th (S) Bn Gloucestershire Regt.

C. Coy.   Left Half Coy: Appendix A
           Operations on Sept. 3.

Half "C" Company worked under 117th Brigade.

No. 11 Platoon was detailed to work from No.1. Sap. No.12 Platoon from No.2. Sap. ½ Coy. H.Q. No.1. Sap.

The Half Company left Camp for Points of Assembly in the Saps at 4.30 p.m. on Sept. 2nd.

"Assembly complete" reported to Brigade at 8.30 p.m. Zero was at 5.10 a.m. Sept. 3rd. Sap exits were 70 yards out in No Man's Land.

The exit of No.2. Sap was under heavy shell fire all day and both ends were several times broken in.

The exit of No.1. Sap was practically free from shell fire, and from it the Infantry were seen advancing and retiring almost immediately, reporting enemy holding front line.

Messages asking for supports were sent back by Infantry through the Sap.

At 7.6 message sent back to Brigade Headquarters stating that work from Sap had not been started as infantry reported enemy holding their front line.

Message from Brigade Headquarters. Time 7.30 a.m "Start work in Sap at once." R.Battalion is in German Trenches also portion of Left."

Message received about 8 a.m. and duplicate about 8.30 a.m.

Message acknowledged 8.35 a.m. as follows:-

"Order received. Work was put in hand on receipt of First Order.

My men have been bombed out of the shell holes they were connecting up. The Sap head itself is completely under Rifle fire from German line. I am commencing a new sap head at entrance to gallery."

At 10.45 a.m. sent message to H.Q. 17th Notts. & Derby's asking if they could tell me who was then holding German line in front of No.1.Sap.

Reply timed 11.30 a.m. "Give no information at all."

3 p.m. Message to Brigade Headquarters: "Am continuing No.1.Sap according to your order B.M/136 AAA O.i/c Sap recommends that my extension should be stopped and the tunnel temporarily blocked with sandbags as long as the enemy is holding his

position opposite and there are no Infantry in our own front line."

Reply timed 3.45 p.m. "You will cease work in the Saps taking care to block up the entrance in order to deny the sap to the enemyAAA After completion of your work you may rejoin your unit."

Half Company completed work and withdrew about 5.30 p.m.

Sgd. H. R. Howman
Major
O.C. C.Coy:
13ᵃ Glos:

Operations September 3rd.

Report from No.9. Platoon, 2nd-Lt. Bennett in charge.

Left Mailly Wood................7.30 p.m. on 2.9.16.
Arrived No.4. Sap in Gordon Trench...1.30 a.m. 3.9.16.
Infantry Attack................5.10 a.m.
    This failed.
2nd Infantry attack............10.30 a.m.
    This failed.
Owing to these failures we carried out no work.

Received order to report at HAMEL about   1 p.m.
      Left Sap................ "   2.30 p.m.
      Arrived Camp............ "   6 p.m.

    Casualties: Reported killed 1 officer.
                     Missing   3 O.R.
                     Wounded   3 O.R.

11.9.16.   (Sgd.) John Davies. Capt.
                        i/c R.½ Company.

Report on work of No.10 Platoon "C" Company,
13th Gloucester Regiment, during operations, 3rd
September, 1916.

No.10 Platoon Left Camp at Mailly Wood at 6.15 p.m.
on 2nd September, 1916, and arrived at assembly place
in valley behind Roberts Trench at 12.45 a.m.
The Platoon was ready to work at the time specified
but owing to the failure of the infantry attack it
was not possible to commence the work of digging a
Communication Trench across No Man's Land.
At about 6 a.m. I communicated with the Officer
Commanding Pioneers in the right sector requesting
further orders. I received a reply informing me that
the attack was at a standstill and was to await
further orders.
Shortly after 2 p.m. I received an order to withdraw
immediately. This was done and with the remainder of
my Platoon I arrived in Camp at 5 p.m. The following
Casualties were sustained: 2 killed, 5 wounded.

(Sd.) S. T. Felstead. 2nd-Lt.

11.9.16.

Pioneers
39th Division.

1/13th BATTALION

GLOUCESTERSHIRE REGIMENT
(pioneers)

OCTOBER 1 9 1 6

WAR DIARY
or
INTELLIGENCE SUMMARY
(Erase heading not required.)

Army Form C. 2118

Vol 8

MAP REFERENCES: FRANCE Sheet 57D. S.E. 1/20000
EDITION 2.D. TRENCH MAP.

Place	Date	Hour	Summary of Events and Information	Remarks and references to Appendices
MAILLY MAILLET	Oct 1,2,3		Work as last month	
"	3	12 noon	Battalion went into billets at ENGLEBELMER.	
ENGLEBELMER	4	4 pm	" " " MARTINSART.	
"	5		A, B + C Coys left for work in the line. Headquarters + D Coy remained.	
			B Coy: clearing dug outs in THIEPVAL (stationed in THIEPVAL, WUNDERWERK and BLIGHTY VALLEY, W.12.c.5.8)	
			A Coy. working on AUTHUILLE – THIEPVAL road (stationed at QUARRY POST, X.1.c.5.a.)	
			C Coy. Laying and repairing tramways from PASSERELLE de MAGENTA across S. CAUSEWAY ast Q.29.c.10.5) (stationed at BLIGHTY VALLEY).	
"	7		Headquarters removed to dug outs at PIONEER ROAD W.10.c.3.8.	
PIONEER Rd ETC	9		D Coy employed on H.T.M. Emplacement in LONGACRE, completing work begun by C Coy last month.	
"	"		A " " dug outs in THIEPVAL and clearing Old German line	
"	11		A and B Coys started communication trench from O.G.L. to Crucifix, approximately R.25.6.2.8 to R.19.d.9.2. (SCHWABEN REDOUBT.)	
"	14	2.45 pm	Attack by 39th Division on SCHWABEN REDOUBT, North face, which still remained in German hands. "A" Coy detailed to consolidate by night, under 234 Field Coy: R.E.	
"	15th	6 a.m.	Attack entirely successful. A Coy returned to QUARRY POST. Lt SAUNDERS' report attached as Appendix A	Appendix A

WAR DIARY
INTELLIGENCE SUMMARY

Army Form C. 2118

Place	Date	Hour	Summary of Events and Information	Remarks and references to Appendices
PIONEER R^D ETC	16th		A Coy employed on Communication trench across SCHWABEN REDOUBT. Other Coys as before	
	17th 18th		Work as usual, much interrupted by shelling.	
	19th		D Coy detailed to consolidate ground gained in proposed attack on STUFF TRENCH. 116 Bde in attack. D Coy attached to this Bde, to work in conjunction with 229 Field Coy. R.E. Operation postponed owing to weather. One platoon "B" Coy attacked to 117 Bde.	
	20th		Further postpone until 21st.	
	21st		Attack took place. Weather fine & clear. Zero hour 12.6 p.m. D Coy in dugouts in THIEP-VAL till evening. C Coy called up to assist D Coy. Attack successful.	
		7.30 pm	Remainder of "B" Coy called on by G.O.C. 117 Bde. for carrying parties.	Appendix B.
		8.30 pm	Detailed report attached as appendix "B"	
	22	6.30 pm	A Coy dug trench from R.19d.9.1 - 8.6. B Coy employed in forming R.E forward dump at R.25.c.2.9 C " " digging trench R.19d.3½.7½ - 9½.7½ (SCHWABEN REDOUBT). Very heavily shelled and dispersed.	
	23.		D Coy: employed in digging trench R.19.c.9.1 - d.2.2 - 4.5.	

Army Form C. 2118

WAR DIARY
INTELLIGENCE SUMMARY
(Erase heading not required.)

Instructions regarding War Diaries and Intelligence Summaries are contained in F.S. Regs., Part II. and the Staff Manual respectively. Title Pages will be prepared in manuscript.

Place	Date	Hour	Summary of Events and Information	Remarks and references to Appendices
PIONEER ROAD etc.	23 Oct	6:30 p.m	A Coy attempted to dig trench R19 d 0.3 – 1.6 – 2.9. Unable to work as R.E. could not locate position.	24/22.
			During the day A & C Coy moved to bivouacs at Headquarters at PIONEER ROAD, B Coy moved one platoon from BLIGHTY VALLEY to LANCASHIRE DUMP.	24 W.
	24/25	night	No working parties owing to wet.	24 W.
	25th	"	B Coy took over work on Tramways. 2 Platoons moved from WUNDERWERK to S. Bluffs near AUTHUILLE.	25 W.
	25/26	night	A & C Coys under R.E. officers attempted to dig trenches near SCHWABEN redoubt. Total failure as points could not be located, shell fire was very heavy and state of ground made any digging impossible. C Coy sustained heavy casualties.	26 W.
	26th		D Coy; employed clearing and metalling AUTHUILLE – THIEPVAL road.	26 W.
	27h		A & C Coys employed laying duck boards from Old British line to O.G.L. under 23rd Coy R.E.	27 W.
	30th		A Coy; worked with 225 Coy R.E. carrying and laying duckboards from O.G.L. to SCHWABEN	30 W.
	31st		Ordinary work.	31 W.

WAR DIARY

INTELLIGENCE SUMMARY

Army Form C. 2118

Place	Date	Hour	Summary of Events and Information	Remarks and references to Appendices
			Casualties for the month.	
			Officers Other Ranks	
			Killed 1 (2Lt P.A. DRAKE) 13	MOSS
			Missing — 1	
			Wounded — 43	
			Died of Wounds — 3	
			Capt: M. Jones awarded MILITARY CROSS on Sept: 28th for gallant conduct on night 3/4 Sept: (omitted in last month's Diary)	MOSS
	1/11/16			
			J.F. Hyme Wilson Major	
			13th Shoreaters.	

Appendix A.

To - C. R. E.,
         39th Division.

From - O.C.,
         13th Gloucester Regt.

With reference to 39th Division R.E. Order No.1. of October 11th, 1916:

In accordance with para.2. of above order, I detailed "A" Company of this Battalion for the work therein mentioned.

One Platoon from this Company was attached to each of the three Sections of the 234 Field Company R.E. The 4th Platoon was kept in reserve.

I have received the following report from Lieut. P. E. H. SAUNDERS, who was in command of "A" Company for these operations:-

Report on Operations 6 p.m. 14.10.16 to 6 a.m. 15.10.16, consolidating SCHWABEN REDOUBT.

5.45 p.m.   Company left QUARRY POST, Nos. 1. and 2. Platoons proceeding via PIP STREET to THIEPVAL to H.Q. 234 Field Coy.R.E. Nos.3. and 4. Platoons proceeded via WOOD POST, OLD GERMAN LINE, and AUTHUILLE and THIEPVAL ROAD to point R.25.c.64. I accompanied the latter party.

6.55 p.m.   I arrived with Nos.3. and 4. Platoons at R.25.c.64. and handed over No.4. to O.C. No.4.Section 234 Field Co.R.E. and placing No.3. Platoon in dugouts at this point in reserve. Enemy had Artillery barrage on AUTHUILLE and THIEPVAL ROAD. We got through without casualties.

7.15 p.m.   I reported personally to Capt. Wood, R.E. at Battn. H.Q. THIEPVAL.

My orders were as follows:

(1) No.2.Platoon to consolidate Point 99 in conjunction with No.2.Section R.E.
(2) No.1.Platoon to consolidate point 69 in conjunction with No.1.Section R.E.
(3) No.4.Platoon to consolidate point 39 in conjunction with No.4.Section R.E.
(4) No.3.Platoon to be in reserve.

7.20 p.m.   My runners with Nos.1.and 2. Platoons reported both platoons handed over to O.Cs.Nos.1.and 2. Sections R.E. at 7 p.m.

7.25 p.m.   I was informed by Capt. Wood that all objectives had been taken with the exception of Point 99. No.2. received orders to proceed as far as possible and and if point not then taken to put in bomb stop where required.

7.30 p.m.   I received an order from Capt.Wood to dig a Communication Trench across the SCHWABEN from Point 65 to near point 69. I detailed No.3.Platoon for this work under 2nd-Lt. Taylor, who was accompanied by an R.E.Officer as guide.

9.0 p.m.   Received information that No.2. were held up by bombing attack on Point 99 and were being heavily shelled. Was informed 2 Coys of K.R.R. had been sent up in support, and at

(2)

9.15 p.m.	that the CAMBRIDGESHIRES were in possession of 99. and that No.2. were proceeding
9.40 p.m.	Report received that No.4. were hung up in OLD GERMAN LINE by Artillery barrage. Orders were sent to party to get forward, which they did. They were informed by O.C. CAMBRIDGESHIRE REGIMENT that no digging was required on right section but that wire was urgently required. The party got all the wire required up to front line, carrying from Dump to the several Companies.
11.10 p.m.	It was reported that all the SCHWABEN was captured and that covering party had pushed out 100 yds in advance of Point 99.
1.50 a.m.	No.3. Platoon was withdrawn, having succeeded in digging over 80 yards of trench across the SCHWABEN to a depth of 5 feet, besides making a journey to the front line with wire.
2.50 a.m.	Withdrew No.4. Platoon, having completed their task as described above.
3.15 a.m.	Recalled No.2. Platoon. This Platoon succeeded in consolidating the right section. The R.E. section failed to arrive (or very few of them) and R.E. Officer was wounded at 1 a.m. 2nd-Lieut. La Trobe was congratulated by O.C. BLACK WATCH for the good work carried out by the Pioneers under at times very heavy fire.
4.50 a.m.	Recalled No.1. Platoon. This Platoon consolidated the centre section very successfully and 2nd-Lieut. Lowe did very good work. This Platoon was under heavy shell fire.
6.0 a.m.	Company arrived QUARRY POST, having been on duty for over 12 hours.

Capt. Wood, R.E., expressed his satisfaction with the work done by the Company and will communicate direct thereon.

I regret to report the following Casualties

Wounded.

18091 Merritt, Sergt. D.W. (slightly)
25102 Balsom, Pte. W.H.
17925 Thomas, " I.
18059 Baigent, Cpl. O.I.
18086 Sheppard, Pte. T.
19569 Fletcher, Pte. H.
19468 Pedley, " I.
26190 Fear, " F.K.
17952 Hall, " H.
17948 Griffiths, " S.E.
19328 Taylor, " A.E.W.

Wounded (Shell Shock).

18662 Acton, Cpl. T.

Missing (believed wounded).

18607 Merry, Pte. G.

(Sd.) P.E.H.Saunders, Lieut.
O.C. "A" Company.

(Sgd) A.H. Boulton Lt.Col.
Cmdg. 13th Gloucester Regt.

15. 10. 16.

Appendix B.

I.

Work of "C" and "D" Companies.

Communication Trench from Point 27 to Point 62 completed to average of 6' cover.
Communication Trench on Right of Sector from BAINBRIDGE TRENCH to Point 85 completed to average of 5' cover.

(Copy sent to H.Q.116 Bde.)

II.

Work of "C" Company. (Detailed report).

Orders were received at 7.30 to be ready to move. O.C. Company reported to G.O.C. 116th Brigade.
The Company moved up at 9 p.m. to assist "D" Coy and 227 Field Coy.R.E. in consolidating STUFF TRENCH. Lt. Drummond was in command.
The Company had never worked in this area, and no guides could be furnished. However Pt.27. was reached, the Company marching by compass and stars.
Nos.9. and 10. Platoons worked with "D" Company to Pt.62.
Nos.11 and 12. Platoons reported to 227 Coy.R.E. at Bn. Headquarters, ZOLLERN TRENCH, after first going to R.20.d.3.5. The men remained there under an officer, while another officer reported to ZOLLERN TRENCH, where he was told that work on the projected centre trench was impossible. These two platoons returned to billets at 4.30 a.m.
Nos. 9. and 10. Platoons returned about 6.30 a.m. having completed the trench from Point 27. to 62. in conjunction with "D" Company. The trench averaged 6' of cover. One Casualty (very slight) was sustained.

III.

Work of No.8. Platoon, "B" Company.
In accordance with Orders from General Staff

39th Division (39/G/28/9/5 of 18.10.16) one platoon of "B" Company was placed at the disposal of the G.O.C. 117th Brigade from Zero hour (12.5) on the day of attack (Oct.21st). No.8. Platoon was detailed under the command of 2nd-Lt.Ryder. They received the order to move at 3.45 p.m. At 4.45 they reported at the Bn. Headquarters of the 16th Rifle Brigade, from there a guide took them to Company Headquarters. Thence they were directed (without guide) to Point 47. They reached this, passing through a heavy barrage, and found it held by a single bomber of the R.B. The fire was too heavy to work on top, and the enemy were seen crawling about 50 yards away, 30 of the men sapped, working in shifts. Two men acted as Guard on the Bombing Post. On the N.E. side of Pt.47, 7-8 yds were dug to a depth of between 4'6" and 5'. On the S.W. side, 4 yds were dug to the same depth. The platoon worked for two hours and twenty minutes, the Company Commander R.B. asking for two hours work. They then reported to Bn. Headquarters of the 16th R.B. and were told to retire, and reached billets at midnight. Casualties, 2 killed, 3 wounded. 2nd-Lt. Ryder brought in a wounded officer (Lt.Clifford) of the 17th Sherwoods from the trench between the bombing blocks.

IV.

Work of Nos. 6 and 7 Platoons, "B" Coy:
These two platoons under 2nd-Lt. Crockford carried Bombs and Ammunition to MARKET TRENCH. There the guides furnished could not find the way to Pt.65. 2nd-Lt. Crockford spent 2½ hours trying this point, but failed. He then deposited the bombs and informed the Brigade Bombing Officer.

V.

Work of No.5.Platoon (Lt. Vowles).

Platoon arrived PAISLEY DUMP about 9.30 p.m. and was kept till 11.30. The guides provided had no idea of the way. Two new guides were provided, and an officer of the Sherwood Foresters, who had been to SCHWABEN redoubt before, accompanied the officer. The Staff Capt. 117th Bde put the officer in charge of 25 machine gunners, as well as his own men. He reached SCHWABEn via MARTIN'S LANE about 1 a.m.. On the way the guide who was leading lost his bearings, and the one with the rear party was brought up. MARTIN'S LANE was very heavily shelled, and the shelling grew more intense towards the SCHWABEN. The men had to lie down in the bottom of the trench. Soon after reaching the SCHWABEN the guide lost his bearings. Lt. Vowles got about a dozen men into a dug out, but found they had lost touch with the rear party. Lt. Vowles and the officer of the Sherwoods tried to find them, but were unable to do so. Lt. Vowles has since found that these men being unable to regain touch, and having no guide, deposited their bombs at the end of MARTIN'S LANE. Lt. Vowles went to Bn. H.Q. in the SCHWABEN and was told to take what stores he had to left Coy. H.Q. which he did (about 1 doz. boxes grenades and 2 doz bandoliers S.A.D.). The Machine Gunners who were in front of the Gloucesters, lost touch. The guides were not satisfactory. I delivered the bombs at 5 a.m.

VI.

Work of "D" Company.

At 5.30 p.m. Capt. Hillier was instructed by G.O.C. 115th Bde. to send his Company to BAINBRIDGE TRENCH to re-dig Communications between this trench and STUFF TRENCH. The two trenches the Company had to re-dig were:-
(a) R.20.d.9.6. - 9.9. - R.21. c.o.9. - R.20.b.8.5.
(b) R.20.a.2.7. - R.20.a.6.2.

Nos.13. and 14. Platoons were ordered to work on (a)
" 15. and 16.   "   "   "   "   "   (b)

Instructions were given that each Platoon should leave a runner at the nearest Bn.H.Q. in the line and that messages should frequently be sent stating progress.

The four Platoons started shortly before 9 p.m.

13 and 14 Platoons reached their work at midnight and were able to finish by 4.45 a.m., shell fire being moderate.

15 and 16 Platoons reached their work at 2 a.m., being held up by a Battalion of Infantry ahead of them.

They completed their work by 5 a.m. without any very heavy shelling.

All Platoons were in Billets by 9 a.m. 22.10.16.

Casualties: 5 wounded.

Pioneers
39th Division.

1/13th BATTALION

GLOUCESTERSHIRE REGIMENT
(pioneers)

NOVEMBER 1 9 1 6

Secret

HEADQUARTERS
A.A. & Q.M.G.
Date 39/1197/A.
No.
39th DIVISION

D.A.G.,
   3rd Echelon.
     BASE.

     Herewith War Diary for the undermentioned Unit, forwarded in continuation of this office No. 39/1197/A dated 11th December 1916 :-

     13th Bn. Gloucestershire Regt.

                               Major-General.
12.12.16.   Commanding 39th Division.

WAR DIARY

INTELLIGENCE SUMMARY

13 Gloucester Vol 9

Army Form C. 2118

Place	Date	Hour	Summary of Events and Information	Remarks and references to Appendices
PIONEER ROAD	Nov. 1st, 2nd, 3rd, 4th		Work as last month.	whas.
	5th		A Coy. worked with 224 Coy. R.E on AUTHUILLE - THIEPVAL road, also erecting huts, repairing screens on road etc. B Coy: continued working tramways C Coy: worked with 234 Coy. R.E., repairing dug-outs, making C.T. across SCHWABEN redoubt, headboarding etc: D Coy worked with 225 Coy R.E clearing extension of INNISKILLING AVENUE across to Pt 91 in O.G.L.	whas.
	6th, 7th, 8th, 9th, 10th, 11th		Work continued as above for Nov 5th	whas.
	12th		All working parties withdrawn by noon. "Y" day	whw. N.

WAR DIARY
INTELLIGENCE SUMMARY
(Erase heading not required.)

Army Form C. 2118

Place	Date	Hour	Summary of Events and Information	Remarks and references to Appendices
PIONEER Bn	Nov 13 "Z" day	4.15 a.m.	Battalion moved out to assembly position (Not Q 3 s d 8.4) in AVELUY WOOD.	cons.
		5.15.	" " in position	eens
		5.45	Zero hour. 39th Division attacked HANSA LINE. Attacking troops were 118th Brigade plus one battalion each from 116th & 117th.	W.W.W.
		10 a.m.	The Battalion moved up for work repairing road from HAMEL to ST PIERRE DIVION, by companies in the order B, A, D, C., the last company moving off at 11.50 a.m. B Coy: started work at 1 p.m.	
		1 p.m.	on making a 4 ft track from Q 24 c. 2.1 to Q 24 c. 8.0. A Coy started work on loop of road	
		1.30 pm	at Q 24 a. 7.0 to Q 24 c. 8.33 at 1.30 p.m. D & C Coys also started work but were very heavily shelled and were obliged to take cover. When the shelling slackened	W.W.W.
		4 p.m.	the road was cleared through to ST PIERRE DIVION. A.D. & C. Coys were ordered to return to billets. B Coy: were ordered, in compliance with instructions for General Staff, 39th Divi, to report to o.c. 1/6th Cheshire Regt at ST PIERRE DIVION, to dig trenches from R.13 c. 7.8 to R.19 c. 6.8 and from R.19 c. 6.8 to R.19 a. 1.8. This Coy: was unable to find the o.c. Bn but dug the trenches under the direction of a Coy Commander 1/6th Cheshires. B Coy: returned to billets at midnight.	
	14th		A Coy: worked on ST P. DIVION road 9 a.m - 1 p.m. Other companies were not sent up as newly received Rat Division were to move out.	leaves.

WAR DIARY

Army Form C. 2118

Instructions regarding War Diaries and Intelligence Summaries are contained in F.S. Regs., Part II. and the Staff Manual respectively. Title Pages will be prepared in manuscript.

INTELLIGENCE SUMMARY
(Erase heading not required.)

Place	Date	Hour	Summary of Events and Information	Remarks and references to Appendices
PIONEER ROAD	Nov 15	12.15pm	Battalion moved to WARLOY.	HQM
LONGUEVILLETTE	16	10 am	Battalion moved to LONGUEVILLETTE via CONTAY & CANDAS	HQM
AUTHEUX	17	10.30 am	Battalion moved to AUTHEUX	HQM
POPERINGHE	18	9.30 am	Battalion moved to DOULLENS & entrained to POPERINGHE	HQM
"		12 M.N	Battalion arrived POPERINGHE & went into billets	HQM
ZEGGERS CAPPEL	19	7 am	Battalion entraining for ESQUELBECQ & marching from there to ZEGGERS CAPPEL went into billets	HQM
"	20		Battalion rest & training at ZEGGERS CAPPEL	HQM
	Dec 1		Battalion moved into the YPRES AREA & took over Pioneer Billets	HQM
	2	12 mn	Battalion moved into billets in the CANAL BANK	HQM
YPRES		8 pm	H.Q. A & D Companies went into billets of LES TROIS TOURS	
			B & C Companies went into Billets	
	18		The following Officers were evacuated during the month of November	HQM
	25		Lt. Col. A.H. Bell when accidentally injured	
			Lt. M.S.C. Drummond sick	
			Casualty report for month Wounded 9 — O.R.	

J.H. Roquier Major
for O.C.
13th G. Unicorns 14/9/4

P.B. 12/10

Headquarters
   39th Division

Herewith report on operations of Nov. 13th as required in your G 390 of 15th.

L. F. Wynne Willson
Major
Cmd 13th Gloucesters.

WARLOY
16/11/16.

Report on Operations 13th Nov 1916.

13th GLOSTERS.

4.15 a.m. The Battalion moved from hutments to their Assembly position (Q 35 d 8.4) in AVELUY WOOD.

5.45 a.m. Zero hour.

10. a.m. The battalion moved up by Companies to repair road HAMEL – ST PIERRE DIVION, in order B, A, D, C.

11.50 a.m. Last Company left Q.35 d 8.4.

1 p.m. B Coy started work making 4 ft track from Q 24 b.2.1. to Q 24 b 8.0.

1.30 p.m. A Coy. started work on road from Q 24 a 7.0 to Q 24 b 3.3.

2.30 p.m. D & C Coy were held up by traffic for some time but started work.
All companies were heavily shelled and work was interrupted.

4 p.m. Road was reported clear for infantry and pack animals to ST PIERRE DIVION. A.C. & D Coys withdrawn to billets.
B Coy:, in accordance with instructions of D.W. General Staff, ordered to report to O.C. 1/6th Cheshires, at ST PIERRE DIVION, to dig trenches from R.13 b 7.8 to R 19 a 6.8. This company was unable to find the O.C. Bn, but reported to an O.C. Coy under whose direction the trenches were dug, and the Coy. returned to billets at midnight.
Bn Casualties – 3 O.R. wounded.

WARLOY
16/11/16.

L. F. Wynne Willson Maj.
O.C. 13th Glos.

Pioneers
39th Division.

1/13th BATTALION

GLOUCESTERSHIRE REGIMENT

(Pioneers)

DECEMBER 1 9 1 6

SECRET

WAR DIARY
or
INTELLIGENCE SUMMARY
(Erase heading not required.)

Army Form C. 2118

1/3 Gloucester
Vol 10

Place	Date 1916	Hour	Summary of Events and Information	Remarks and references to Appendices
YPRES	Dec 2		Battalion having relieved 1/4th Welsh (Pioneers) continues their work as follows:—	
			"A" Company. Extension of GOWTHORPE ROAD & new trench CONEY ST to GOWTHORPE & Dugouts in CANAL BANK	
			"B" " Making new front line between SKIPTON CT & EALING CT Repairing COLNE VALLEY CT Improving billets at TROIS TOURS	
			"C" " Repairing ESSEX TRENCH Reclaiming X LINE in L Brigade sector in L Brigade sector Improving billets at TROIS TOURS	
			"D" " Cleaning & repairing CAVAN DRAIN Reclaiming FORWARD TRENCH from CROSS ROADS FARM to FORWARD COTTAGE & Burbury Dugouts in CANAL BANK	
	19		"B" " Handed over part of their work in EALING to "C" Coy & took over the same on Gravenvel front & drew out Burbs for working this from system which was passed by C.R.E.	
			"C" " Bgan approach tunnel to LES TROIS TOURS by order of CRE	

WAR DIARY
or
INTELLIGENCE SUMMARY

(Erase heading not required.)

Army Form C. 2118

Place	Date 1916	Hour	Summary of Events and Information	Remarks and references to Appendices
YPRES	Dec 27		"A" Coy stopped work on CANAL BANK CUT & DRAIN. Dugouts began to work on DAWSON. "C" Coy started a dugout at TROIS TOURS, for the Signal Cables also a dugout for the APM & a cage for prisoners. Casualties for month 1 OR died of wounds 2/Lt H. Eaton joined the Battalion from No 33 IBD 23-12-16	AP24 14P24 16P24 14P24

H.A. Stephens Major
for Lt. Col. 13th Gloucesters.

66TH DIVISION TRAINING CADRES

39 DIV
(PIONEERS)

13TH BN GLOSTER REGT.
~~SEP - DEC 1918~~

191̶8̶ 7 Sept to 1919 MAY

FROM 39 DIV TROOPS

Served with 197 Bde
L of C from Sept 1918
ONWARDS

WAR DIARY
or
INTELLIGENCE SUMMARY

1/3 Gloucester R.E.

Army Form C. 2118

(Erase heading not required.)

Vol XI

Place	Date	Hour	Summary of Events and Information	Remarks and references to Appendices
YPRES	June 1915			
	7		The Battalion continued the work begun in December	HQW
			"A" Coy started defences BOAR LANE from the WILLOWS southwards	HQW
			"D" Coy started retaining & draining the C.T. from HILLTOP FARM to SIEGE TRENCH	HQW
	9	2 pm	POPERINGHE was shelled for the first time for some months	HQW
	10	4:30pm	The Billets of the detachment ("B"&"C" Coys) at LES TROIS TOURS were shelled for the first time. One shell which fell close to the hut occupied by "B" Coy signallers was responsible for 13 casualties (2 killed & 11 wounded). The incident was kept damaged.	HQW
	11		Orders having been received to the effect that the Battalion would move into the 53rd Brunswood area (on the R) on Jun 14th Coy officers made a reconnaissance of the work of the 1/4 Sth N.F.S (Pioneers) & advance parties of "C" & "D" Coys went over that night to occupy billets vacated by 1/4 So Lancs.	HQW
	12	2 pm	Coy conferences of 1/19th Welch (Pioneers) arrived without weapons at TROIS TOURS	HQW
	13		Strong advance parties of "A" & "B" Coys were sent to occupy billets vacated by 1/4 So Lancs.	HQW & Sheet 10N
	14		HQ & the remainder of the Battalion moved & occupied billets	HQW Sheet

WAR DIARY
or
INTELLIGENCE SUMMARY
(Erase heading not required.)

Army Form C. 2118

Place	Date	Hour	Summary of Events and Information	Remarks and references to Appendices
YPRES	Jany 1917		as follows. H.Q. + "D" Coy at BRANDHOEK. "A" "B" & "C" in the town of YPRES.	WDH
	15		Work was started as follows:- "A" Coy repairing reclaiming PICCADILLY, WEST LANE, & MUD LANE C.T.s "B" Coy took over the drainage of the Divisional area reusing Tub platoons for work on HAYMARKET C.T. "C" Coy started work on GARDEN CITY, NEW JOHN ST & STRAND CTs "D" Coy refloaring the Billets at BRANDHOEK which had been badly neglected by the outgoing unit	WDH
	17		Coys: were detailed to work as follows - A Coy under 225 Coy. R.E. (Right Forward Sector) C Coy " " 234 " " (Left " ") B Coy Drainage and BELLEWAARDE BEEK D Coy at H.Q.	LAWS
	22/23		D Coy relieved A Coy.	LAWS
	30/31		A " " B Coy	LAWS

WAR DIARY
or
INTELLIGENCE SUMMARY
(Erase heading not required.)

Army Form C. 2118

Place	Date	Hour	Summary of Events and Information	Remarks and references to Appendices
			Casualties for month O.R. 3 Killed. 1 missing 2 died of wounds 16 wounded. The following Honours & Awards appeared in the NEW YEAR honours mentioned - D.S.O. Lt Col. A.H. Paulton Capt. W.M. de Paula "Lt" S.M. Henryman Lt Col. A.H. Boulton D.S.O. Military Medal Pte 19426 Cpl. W. Chant (D Coy) 20253 Pte J. Smith (C Coy) The following officers joined the Battalion. 9th 2/Lt E.G. Richards, J. Clae, to Remington 16th " A.V. Burch, W.L. Taylor 23rd " E.M. Kennard, 24th " A.F. Hall, G. Wrighton 2nd Lt S. Henryman was transferred to the R.F.C. on the 11th.	2/9th W L. Wynne Hatton attd only 13th Gloucesters.

SECRET

Army Form C. 2118

13 Gloucester Reg[t]
Vol 12

WAR DIARY or INTELLIGENCE SUMMARY

(Erase heading not required.)

Instructions regarding War Diaries and Intelligence Summaries are contained in F.S. Regs., Part II and the Staff Manual respectively. Title Pages will be prepared in manuscript.

11. N.
2 sheets

Place	Date 1917	Hour	Summary of Events and Information	Remarks and references to Appendices
YPRES	7/8		Relieved C.	Ref
	17		Handed over to 1/4 S. LANCS	Ref
	17/18		Bn. marched to billets in POPERINGHE	Ref
	18	10·30 am	Bn. entrained at CHEESE MARKET for ZEGGERS CAPPEL - detrained about 1·30 pm	Ref
	23		C.O. and Adjutant - to YPRES to arrange relieving return from 9th S.STAFFS 23rd DIV.	Ref
	24		Advance parties from B.C. and D. Coys to YPRES by lorry	Ref
	25		B and C Coys entrained at ZEGGERS CAPPEL for YPRES and relieved B and C Coys 9th S. STAFFORDS	Ref
	26		A and D Coys and H.Q. entrained for YPRES to relieve remainder of S.STAFFS 23 A Coy attached 2nd CANADIAN TUNNELLING COY 39th DIVISION transferred to X CORPS Officers serving: 2nd Lt QUINTON D.P. 6th Glos. 2nd Lt BEEL W.D. 20th Glos. 2nd Lt FARR. L.C. 2nd Glos. 2nd Lt PAWSEY J.S. 2/6 Glos. LT DEWE C.D.E. 2nd Glos. LT HILLIER G.S.D. 20th Glos.	Ref

Place	Date	Hour	Summary of Events and Information	Remarks and references to Appendices
YPRES	10/17		Casualties for month:- Wounded 3 O.R. Wounded Gassed 6 O.R. Died of wounds 1 O.R.	

M Sanders Capt
for O.C. 18 Queens
29th Oct 1917

WAR DIARY or INTELLIGENCE SUMMARY

Army Form C. 2118

13 Glouc Regt

Vol 13

Place	Date 1917	Hour	Summary of Events and Information	Remarks and references to Appendices
YPRES	May		HQ billets in RAMPARTS near LILLE GATE	A/M
			A Coy at RENINGHELST attached to 2nd CANADIAN TUNNELING COY	
			B " " INFANTRY BARRACKS	
			C " " CAVALRY "	
			D " " " "	
			C+D Coy were heavily shelled causing casualties.	
			WORK	
			B Coy Improved Tramways.	
			C " Protecting billets & erecting Elephant dugouts in CAVALRY BARRACKS & near C.T. ARNAGH WOOD Southward from	A/M
			STAFFORD ST.	
			D " New C.T. from ZILLEBEKE ST to STAFFORD ST	A/M
	6		A " Left the Tunneling Coy were billeted at DEVISIONAL REINFORCEMENT CAMP.	A/M
	7		" " WORK new C.T. STAFFORD ST to HALIFAX	A/M
	12		" " moved to YPRES & billeted at INFANTRY BARRACKS & RAMPARTS	A/M
	14		HQ heavily shelled, casualties caused	A/M

12.N
2 sheet

Army Form C. 2118

WAR DIARY
or
INTELLIGENCE SUMMARY
(Erase heading not required.)

Instructions regarding War Diaries and Intelligence Summaries are contained in F.S. Regs., Part II. and the Staff Manual respectively. Title Pages will be prepared in manuscript.

Place	Date 1917	Hour	Summary of Events and Information	Remarks and references to Appendices
YPRES	Mch 22	6.30–8 pm	N.2. heavily shelled	MOA
	24	5.30–6 pm	" " " one deep dugout damaged	MOA
	26	1–2 pm	" " " main gallery blown in	MOA
	26	10.30 pm	N.2. moved to transport lines	MOA
	29		N.2. moved into CAVALRY BARRACKS YPRES	MOA
				MOA
			CAPTAIN E.T. BURR appointed Staff Captain to Fourth Army (Auth. MACA/20866) increase of establishment	MOA
			approved by MS general list on increase of establishment & Communication NO124 dated	MOA
			11/2/17. A.G.B. List of appointments & Communication NO124 dated 24/2/17.	
			CAPT J.F DAVIS to England sick 13/3/17.	
			Lt Col A.H. BOULTON Rejoins Battalion 4/3/17.	
			Casualties for month.	
			Killed 7 OR	
			Died of wounds 4 "	
			Wounded 27 "	MOK

[signature] Major
for O.C. 13 h Gloucesters
31/3/17.

1875 Wt. W593/826 1,000,000 4/15 J.B.C. & A. A.D.S.S./Forms/C. 2118.

WAR DIARY

INTELLIGENCE SUMMARY

(Erase heading not required.)

Army Form C. 2118

13 Gloucester R¹
for 1.4

Place	Date 1917	Hour	Summary of Events and Information	Remarks and references to Appendices
YPRES	April 6		"A" & "C" Companies started rivet work on WALL OF CHINA. Digging three drains & putting new C.T. called OXFORD STREET between GORDON HOUSE	
	9		Remains of 7 men of CATHEDRAL YPRES removed by RE	
	9	7.30	Battalion "Stood to" in billets for an hour during enemy attack on R SECTOR	
	12		"D" Coy moved to D. CAMP to build new DIVISIONAL. HQ.	
	17		HQ moved to D CAMP	
			"A" & "C" Companies moved to CANAL BANK & took over work from 19th WELSH	
			"B" Coy moved into Billets at RUBROUKY	
	20		"A" Coy started constructing new trench behind BILGE TRENCH from the N	
			"C" " " " " " " " BILGE TRENCH " S	
			"A" " " " CT between GOWTHORPE & CONEY ST	
			"C" " " " CT between McGREGORS POST & TOWER POST	
	26		A & B Companies changed Billets & Work	
	29		D Coy started constructing DUGOUTS on CANAL BANK with Infantry Labour	
	25		Casualties for the month. Wounded in action 4. O.R.	

2/Lt R.V. RYDER Transferred to RFC 18/4/17 authority AOS No 2030/2/143 dated 13.4.17
MAJOR. L.F. WYNNE-WILLSON having been instructed being found unfit to return. Medical Boards dated (W.O.A.C.4427.2.17) struck off strength of Battalion accordingly
2/Lt J. CLOSE to ENGLAND 2/3.17 (28 days with leave granted by G.H.Q.)

H.A.H. Hardman Major
13th R¹ Gloucesters
for CO.

13.11
1 sheet

Army Form C. 2118

WAR DIARY
or
INTELLIGENCE SUMMARY

13 Gloucester Rgt.

Oct /15

(Erase heading not required.)

Instructions regarding War Diaries and Intelligence Summaries are contained in F.S. Regs., Part II. and the Staff Manual respectively. Title Pages will be prepared in manuscript.

Place	Date 1915	Hour	Summary of Events and Information	Remarks and references to Appendices
CANAL BANK YPRES	MAY 1/31		"A" Coy carried on work on BILGE TRENCH, S. + FINCH STREET on return from Back Area	
			"B" Coy " " " BILGE TRENCH N + GILLSON ST	140/4
			"C" Coy " " " BILGE TR. S. + FINCH ST until relieved by A.	140/4
			"D" Coy " " " dug trench to CANAL BANK and tramway on BUFFS RD	140/4
	12		A Coy from Back Area at RUBROUCK relieving C Coy	140/4
	24		"C" Coy moved to D Coy's + "D" Coy to CANAL BANK	
	18/20		"A" + "B" Coys dug, wired + camouflaged BELLINGHAM TRENCH	
	26/27		A, B + D Coys dug ARMYTAGE TRENCH	
			C Coy dug GARDEN ST	
	27/30		C+D Coys wired + hurt branches ARMYTAGE TRENCH.	140/4.
			Casualties for the month NIL	

A Thomson Major
for C.O. 13th Gloucesters.

WAR DIARY

Army Form C. 2118

INTELLIGENCE SUMMARY 13th (FOREST OF DEAN) BATT. GLO'STER REGt

(Erase heading not required.)

Place	Date	Hour	Summary of Events and Information	Remarks and references to Appendices
CANAL BANK YPRES	1917 Nov		During the month the following New Trenches were completed By "A" Cy, HALL C.T., CLARK C.T., & the new part of BILGE to CONEY ST By "B" Cy, GILLSON ST to HORNBY By "C" Cy, FINCH ST from McGREGORS POST to BILGE "D" Cy, Constantly increased DUGOUT accommodation on E. Bank of CANAL. "B","C"+"D"Cys. joined up POSTS from C.14.1 to C.14.4 making it possible to move along this part of the FRONT LINE in daylight.	
	6/7		"C"+HQ. Coy. moved to CANAL BANK from D. CAMP D. Coy. moved to C CAMP, C Coy being in their DUGOUTS in E. BANK of CANAL	
	16.		A & B Coy took over DUGOUTS occupied by 19th WELSH	
	23		A & C Coy dug HORNBY C.T. to junction of GILLSON ST. This work was considerably delayed by heavy rain.	
	26/30		All work was much delayed during the month by continuous SHELL FIRE on C.Ts + also on the Work. Our working parties were fired on by ENEMY AIRCRAFT. CANAL BANK was shelled frequently thereby causing damage to DUGOUTS + casualties. Our GUNS did not appear to make any reply	

15 N 2 sheets

WAR DIARY

INTELLIGENCE SUMMARY

13th (FOREST OF DEAN) BATT. GLO'STER REGT.

Army Form C. 2118

Place	Date	Hour	Summary of Events and Information	Remarks and references to Appendices
CANAL BANK YPRES	June		Casualties for the month Offr. O.R. Killed — 3 Wounded 1 24 x died of wounds — 1 x includes 5 O.R. at duty 2/Lt WEST R.P.H joined Bn 15-6-17 " DENNIS L.C. " 18-6-17 Capt JONES H wounded in action 26.6.17.	MK

J.H. Stroman Major
for O.C. 13th Gloucesters
30-6-17

WAR DIARY or INTELLIGENCE SUMMARY

Army Form C. 2118

Place	Date 1917	Hour	Summary of Events and Information	Remarks and references to Appendices
CANAL BANK YPRES	30/7 28/7 29"		Bn. employed on completion of recently trenches, maintenance of C.T.s and fire trenches, construction of trench tramway and dug-outs into a mine to defensive operations.	
	1/8		B. Coy detached to report for instruction in railway construction to A.D.L.R. XVIII CORPS	
	29/8		Bn (less B Coy detached) withdrawn to C Brigade Group of Canfo	
	NIGHT 30/31		Bn (less one Coy) returned to CANAL BANK arriving about 2 a.m. (Zero hour 3.50am) S.H.P.	
	31st 2am		Bn (less one Coy) detailed to report to O.C.s R.E. & ADMIRALS RD. (ST JULIEN RD. 20.V.W. 2. C. 22. c. 7.6) to its junction with the WIELTJE - ST JULIEN RD.	
	5.45am		Bn. received orders to move forward from C.T. Div. Reserve Control and finish shift.	
	12 noon		(13th & 32nd O.R.) was seen at CANAL BANK at 6.57 a.m. BUFFS RD reported fit for field guns from ADMIRALS RD to junction to new W of old German front line.	
	2pm		Second shift (2nd & 34th O.R.) left CANAL BANK, returning from shift 2.45 pm	
	4pm		First shift returned CANAL BANK - Reported roads 15'0" wide clear from ADMIRALS RD to junction of BUFFS RD and WIELTJE - ST JULIEN RD.	
	11pm		Second shift returned to CANAL BANK. Reported damage from shells and bombs	

WAR DIARY
or
INTELLIGENCE SUMMARY

Army Form C. 2118

(Erase heading not required.)

Instructions regarding War Diaries and Intelligence Summaries are contained in F.S. Regs., Part II. and the Staff Manual respectively. Title Pages will be prepared in manuscript.

Place	Date 1917	Hour	Summary of Events and Information	Remarks and references to Appendices
CANAL BANK YPRES	JULY 30	2 a.m.	Parties of permanent cadres and all working during the day, and 4 min. blew up in road about 60 yds W of road junction at C.23.a.4.2. Working two men.	
			Casualties: Lieut. Kelly & VR—wounded 23 VR.	
		31st	B Coy employed on light railway work under A.D.L.R. refuting Casualties 23 VR. Casualties for month — killed 2. 2/Lt FRAMPTON 3 R. 32/717 VR.14	
			2/Lt EATON H. 31.4.117 VR. 2	
			Missing believed wounded U/O U/R 2	
			Killed U/O U/R 68 (8 or etc.)	
			Wounded U/O U/R 2	
			Died of wounds U/O V.R. 4	
			Gassed O/O V.R. 2	
			Sent from shell eyes	
		10th	2/Lt FARNDELL (R) (U) joined Bn.	
		12th	Severely increased activity in the front & trench systems during the month especially on the use of new light & gas shell enclosures to mustard oil	
			LT. COL. A. H. BOUTON attended 19th G.A.	AWARDS
			2/Lt NEWARD, E.W. to September 19th ... 14954 Sgt. J.W. BUFFREY	
			LATROBE. F.H. ... 20230 Pte G. STEVENS	
			WRIGHTON G. ... 7701 AVERY L.W.	
			DENNIS S.G. Graduated musketry course at Aldershot 19/8th Awarded MM to G.S.X??	

Signed
Lt Col Cmd'g

13 Gloucestershire Vol 18

WAR DIARY
or
INTELLIGENCE SUMMARY
(Erase heading not required.)

Army Form C. 2118

Instructions regarding War Diaries and Intelligence Summaries are contained in F.S. Regs., Part II. and the Staff Manual respectively. Title Pages will be prepared in manuscript.

Place	Date 1917	Hour	Summary of Events and Information	Remarks and references to Appendices
CANAL BANK YPRES	Aug 1-4		Bn less one Coy employed repairing and widening BUFFS RD from ADMIRALS RD to junction with WIELTJE - ST JULIEN RD	(1)
VLAMERTINGHE	5th		Bn less one Coy moved back into bivouacs near VLAMERTINGHE and handed over work to 5th Bn R. SUSSEX REG. (PIONEERS)	(2)
BERTHEN	8th	noon	Bn less one Coy entrained at VLAMERTINGHE for CAESTRE. Thence by route to BERTHEN area (by bus)	(3)
VIERSTRAAT	15th		Bn less one Coy moved by lorry from BERTHEN to VIERSTRAAT and took over new bivouacs with from 19 Bn MIDDLESEX REG (PIONEERS)	(4)
"	16th		Bn less one Coy moved up with from 19 Bn A.D.L.R.	
"	17th		B. Coy reconnoitered the Bn front:— Coy employed as under:—	
			A – repairing & deepening UAF AVENUE C.T.	
			B – Repairing road Gada	
			C – Installing Flash board metres X CORPS	
			D – Repairing UPTIC AVE C.T. and made a diversion with the diggings to IMPERIAL AVE C.T.	
			CASUALTIES: Wounded O.R 11 (details)	
			Gas & wounds O.R 2	
			AWARDS: 15116 Sgt H. VAUGHAN	
			11907 T. DORRINGTON (M.M. Gaz XVIII Corps)	
			17896 Pte F. CLIFTON	
			17613 " W.G. BROWN	
	19th		H.Q. Gilbert M.C. formed 9th Bn. Reg.	

1875. W. W593/826 1,000,000 4/15 J.B.C. & A. A.D.S.S./Forms/C.2118.

Army Form C. 2118

WAR DIARY
or
INTELLIGENCE SUMMARY

13 Gloucesters [?]

(Erase heading not required.)

Instructions regarding War Diaries and Intelligence Summaries are contained in F. S. Regs., Part II. and the Staff Manual respectively. Title Pages will be prepared in manuscript.

Place	Date	Hour	Summary of Events and Information	Remarks and references to Appendices
VIERSTRAAT	SEPT. 1917		A, C, D Coys employed on road repairs, and the formation of mule tracks in conjunction with active operations in SHREWSBURY FOREST in Sept. 26th. the capture of TOWER HAMLETS on Sept. 26th. D Coy employed on laying and maintaining trench tramway in same area.	
S2 & 50 Sheet 28 BELGIUM / FRANCE	29th		Bn. withdrawn to IX Corps area for rest - on the Division being withdrawn from the line. Casualties for month: Offrs O.R. Killed or missing — 7 Died of wounds — 1 Wounded — 35* +(includes gas-casualties) Honours and Awards:- T/Capt P.E.H. SAUNDERS awarded M.C. (D.R.O. 4.9.17) W.T. BROWN RAMC M.C. do. LT. COL. A.H. BOULTON D.S.O. struck off strength (Medical Board wounds). A.G. No.D/10813 2/LT J.G. PAVLING to England 11.9.17 (accidentally injured)	

[signatures]
Lt. Col.
O.C. 13th Gloucesters
30/9/17

SECRET

WAR DIARY
or
INTELLIGENCE SUMMARY.
(Erase heading not required.)

Army Form C. 2118.

13 Gloucester R.
Oct 20

Place	Date 1917	Hour	Summary of Events and Information	Remarks and references to Appendices
LOCRE	Oct 2		Battalion went "A" in ground into huts at LOCRE worked on trees strongpoints	
			Lewis Coys. A Coy went into camp near BRASSERIE tanks & cookers & Coys	
			to MORLAND AVENUE	N/A
VIERSTRAAT	16		Battalion occupied BODEZONNE FARM	N/A
	17		and commenced work on NORTHERN TRACK	N/A
	22		Stopped work on NORTHERN TRACK. Began on PLUMER'S DRIVE under X Corps	N/A
			Transport Officer Lieut BODEZONNE FARM for new draft. (50 O.R's)	
	27		Relieved from Trenches by 10th Camp Battn DURNFELD & LOCK 8	N/A
	28		And again started work on NORTHERN TRACK	
	30			
			Casualties for month	
			Killed 1 O.R.	
			Wounded 7 O.R.	
			LT COL A.H. BOULTON joined 17.10.17 from sick leave	
			2/LT A.H. RICHE joined 1.10.17 on appointment	
			2/LT H.B. HARVEY " " 19.10.17	
			CAPT H.D. HILLIER & 2/LT F.B. WHITTALL proceeded to ENGLAND for 6 months Rest work.	N/A
			Adm GHQ No A/209 (O.J) of 4.10.17	
			2/LTS. A.C. BAKER. V.S. BERRY. F.B. WHITTALL. R. HOLLAND. H. LOWE M.C. H.G. REECE.	

19.N
2 visit

Army Form C. 2118.

WAR DIARY
or
INTELLIGENCE SUMMARY.
(Erase heading not required.)

Instructions regarding War Diaries and Intelligence Summaries are contained in F.S. Regs., Part II. and the Staff Manual respectively. Title pages will be prepared in manuscript.

Place	Date	Hour	Summary of Events and Information	Remarks and references to Appendices
			A/S CROCKFORD M.C. CMJJERVIS. Appointed Temp. Lieuts. 1.7.16 (?) Temp. Lieut. Ig 18 wants Maurices	147A
			Lt C.M.JJERVIS proceeded to ENGLAND 22.10.17 pending evacuation to INDIA for passage to Indian Army.	148A
			T/MAJOR H.R. HOWMAN M.C. acting Lt Col. whilst commanding Bttalion 28.7.17	149A
			T/CAPT W.N. de PAULA M.C. to Acting MAJOR whilst employed as 2 In Comd 28.7.17 Apps told No 150 M/25.8.17.	150A

[signature]

For OC 13th Gloucesters
23/10/17

Army Form C. 2118.

13 Bato (Pauy) br.

WAR DIARY
INTELLIGENCE SUMMARY.
(Erase heading not required.)

Place	Date 1917	Hour	Summary of Events and Information	Remarks and references to Appendices
VOORMEZEELE	1 Nov		Work on MULE TRACK called GLOUCESTER DRIVE etc continued throughout	AF/14
	2/3		comp'd to MR Bn H.Qs. E of DUNBARTON LAKES.	AF/14
	11		C & D Coys started work on BUMERS DRIVE under CORPS	AF/14
	16		C, D Coys started to work C.T. to MENIN ROAD	AF/14
YPRES N.24	23		H.Q, A & E Coys moved to SALVATION CORNER	AF/14
	25		B & D "	AF/14
	26		Battalion started work under VIII Corps repairing, reclaiming & extending forward tracks towards PASSCHENDAELE & A Cpl erected The Pilchard for SPREE FARM water front	
			Casualties for month killed 1 O.R. wounded 29 O.R (including 3 at duty)	AF/14
			7/MAJOR H.R.HOMAN relinquishes the acting rank of Lt Col on ceasing to command Bn 18/10/17	AF/14
			7/CAPT W.M de PAULA M.C " Major on ceasing to be employed as 2/IC 18/10/17	AF/14

W.H. Mannantheijm
for Lt Col 13 M.G.November 30/11/17.

Army Form C. 2118.

13 Gloucester
Pgs 1 22

WAR DIARY
or
INTELLIGENCE SUMMARY.
(Erase heading not required.)

Instructions regarding War Diaries and Intelligence Summaries are contained in F. S. Regs., Part II. and the Staff Manual respectively. Title pages will be prepared in manuscript.

Place	Date	Hour	Summary of Events and Information	Remarks and references to Appendices
	1917			
YPRES N. Sect.	7		A B & C Coys inflicted on construction of new (flash) road from ZONNEBEKE to SEINE	
			and D Coy on road repairs between FREZENBERG and ZONNEBEKE (under VIII Corps)	
CAGNE	9		Bn entrained at YPRES — ASYLUM STATION — for STEENWOORDE & billeted	
BURDINGHILLE	10		Bn billeted at GODEWAERSVELDE (in DEBRIES) — Area E WILLE J. BURDINGHILLE	
(UMBRES) CAZ			— [illegible] and training — (X Corps Army)	
	24		Bn proceeded by route march to HABLETTES	
	30		Bn proceeded by march route to WIZERNES and [illegible] of EVERDINGHE	
			with 116 Brigade Group — Horses & Wheeled transit to SIEGES CAMP	
			Lt E L DERRIE L.G. Employed Signals [illegible] TANK CORPS (attd with ABM/G/B/4/17 dated 13/11/17)	
	22		2/Lt REMINGTON to relieved posthumous from [illegible] duties [illegible] [illegible] & New Zealand	
Moulins en Trompaides (Provisional Pas d. C.)			[illegible] Pr. 1 dt 22/11/17] Maj R Bowman. Cpl— BSD Hillier ha[illegible] [illegible]	
			Capt. O.J— (Army) 2/Lt R de Paiva M.C. to told May with effect 19-2-17 Old W-[illegible] 107/	
Remainder at			T/Lt (7 Cpt.) G.S.D.Hiller to told Capt. with effect — 26/11/17 {8862 (M&V 4) of 26/11/17}	
			T/Lt HA VOYLES L.G of M/Cs — (actual), 28/10/17 — Adl. A G letter 118 of 2/11/17)	
			2/Lt GW Farrington 13/12/17 Pabl 3 Cy off [signature] 2/c [illegible]	
			P/Lt D D HERRING 19/12/17	

13 E.Yorks R.

Army Form C. 2118

WAR DIARY
or
INTELLIGENCE SUMMARY.

(Erase heading not required.)

22N
2 sheets

Place	Date	Hour	Summary of Events and Information	Remarks and references to Appendices
	1918			
EVERDINGHE	Jan 1 to 20		Battalion in Hutment Lits at SIEGE CAMP. B.H.Q. at FANTASID FARM.	A.H.R.
			Battalion worked in CORPS LINE North East of ST JULIEN, practicing same — digging and revetting drain.	M.R.
PROVEN	21		Battalion moved by march Route into Huts and Tents at POMPEY CAMP, PROVEN	M.R.
CHIGNOLLES	26		Battalion entrained for MERICOURT L'ABBÉ and marched thence to MARLEY CAMP, CHIGNOLLES (Somme)	M.R.
HAUT ALLAINES	30		Battalion marched to camp at HAUT ALLAINES	M.R.
			Casualties for month:-	
			O.R. Killed 1, missing 2, wounded 5 (1st at duty).	
			Following Officers joined Battalion on appointment from 2nd E.R. Wingfield 2nd Lieut L.Myors	
			S.J.M.Birch & Taylor Rejoined 2/Lt. F.W.Wilkinson 15.1.18.	
			Departures. Capt P.R.H. Saunders M.C. posted to England to duty with Land Corps (A/4/49/) A.D.	
			127 (D) Bn 29.12.17	
			Lt. J. Barry to the front 13.12.17	
			2/Lt to throw in low (alt source 3rd March) Released from Building Detail	

Lt. J. Barry

Army Form C. 2118.

WAR DIARY
or
INTELLIGENCE SUMMARY.
(Erase heading not required.)

Place	Date	Hour	Summary of Events and Information	Remarks and references to Appendices
			in order to count Indian States (2 Queen Regt / 1324 / m S.I.T.) m 15.12.17	
			Lt. J.J. Robinson. Inlisted 9.1.18 Granted 21 days sick leave	K.R.
			by S.M.O.B. Rept. 31.1.18	
			Lt. Col. C. H. Boulton D.S.O. d. Hq 20.1.18	
			M. Worth Cpt.	
			for F.E. 13th Bn. Worcester Regt	
			31.1.18.	

Army Form C. 2118.

WAR DIARY
of
INTELLIGENCE SUMMARY.
(Erase heading not required.)

23 N.
3 sheets

Place	Date 1918	Hour	Summary of Events and Information	Remarks and references to Appendices
GOUZEAUCOURT	1/4		Battalion returned to Camp in SOREL LE GRAND & took over tents from Royal Bucks g.R. Division	A24
	2		Battalion started work on Main Line of Resistance (RED LINE) from POSTAL to POSTAL14. Work consisted of (a) constructing trench & accommodation for personnel (b) forming up of Lewis gun posts	A24
	2/3	night	Half the Battle occupies 172 bn Batt on the Bde Reserve Line	A24
			G METHUEN TRENCH & received congratulations of G.O.C. Division on occupying Bde in the given time allotted	A24
	4/5	night	130 O.R. members 118 Inf. Bde by instructing & arrived from about R.26.a.7 to about R.26.a.9.R.8	A24
	27		Battalion started work on YELLOW LINE (OUTPOST & SUPPORT) constructing trenches from to Tortuary of intention	A24
	27/28	night	Bde returned completed intelligence turning over lines from CHAPEL CROSSING to cancel TRENCH	A24
	28/29	night	Survey through the R.M.F.A. modified the replacement of 1st Engineers	A24
			J. NURLU, SOREL LE GRAND & HEUDECOURT	

Army Form C. 2118.

WAR DIARY
or
INTELLIGENCE SUMMARY.
(Erase heading not required.)

Place	Date	Hour	Summary of Events and Information	Remarks and references to Appendices
			Casualties for the month	
			Mormal. 1. O.R.	
			The following Officers were transferred to the Battn from 14 "B"	WOH
			Res. Bn. 11.2.18 in accordance with S.A.G.S. and A.F. No S/707415 of 31/1/18	
			Capt E.J.L. SHUFFLEBOTHAM MC T/2/Lt E.N.H. RUST	
			" F.E.A. BERGER-WALLER " R.N. ANDERSON	
			Lt A.M.B. DANNE " R.G. LEE	
			T/2/Lt E.J. RUNDLE M.C. D.C.M. 2/Lt L.A. WILMOTT	
			" F.J. LOVELL " W.H.C. HOMER MC	
			" A.E. HOLBOROW T " A.B. CALCOTT	WOH
			The following Officers joined the Battalion	
			Lt. COL A.H. BOULTON DSO from sick leave 10.2.18	
			2/Lt F.S. SMITH from I.B.D. 22.2.18	WOH
			Admitted to Hospital 1 2/Lt F.J. RUNDEE MC DCM 15.2.18 G.S.W. face	
			Received in return whilst serving with 14th S/oro.	WOH

WAR DIARY
INTELLIGENCE SUMMARY

Army Form C. 2118.

Appointments.

T/Major H.R. Hawman A/L/t of Lt Col Shield commanding
Batt. 26/1/18. A.G's List 174 10.2.18.

" LONDON GAZETTE from G Capt. P.E.H. Saunders awarded M.C.

" 2/Lt F.H. LaTrobe, M.C. to be T/Lt 30 Oct 17.

" Jan 15 - T/Lt C.W. Jervis from A to R to T/Lt on appt.
as adjt to 2nd Army. Rkg of off 26 Nov 17.

" Jan 22. T/Lt H.H. Vowles to be A/Capt (adjt) 25 Oct 17

" Jan 1 T/Capt. H.D. Hillier } Awarded M.C.
T/Capt. J.C. Procter }

V.R. Hawman Major
for O.C. 13 Bn Gloucester R.
1 March 1918

Pioneers.
39th Div.

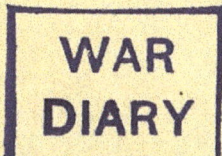

13th BATTN. THE GLOUCESTERSHIRE REGIMENT.

M A R C H

1 9 1 8

WAR DIARY or INTELLIGENCE SUMMARY

Army Form C. 2118.

39/3 Gloucester Vol 25

Place	Date 1918	Hour	Summary of Events and Information	Remarks and references to Appendices
CARDENCOURT	March 1/12		Battalion carried on work on the YELLOW & BROWN LINES of defence	1/13/4
SECTOR				
BEAUMETZ	12		Battalion moved to BEAUMETZ whilst 9 work on the GREENLINE made by XIX Corps	11/3/4
	21/2		Battalion moved to TEMPLEUX LA FOSSE to carry out attack with 39th Div later Reserve. Same night Battn. joined with other troops in the line LONGAVESNES - SAULCOURT	11/33
	22/3		Battalion moved to reoccupied an Enemy in GREEN LINE E.g. TEMPLEUX LA FOSSE X	11/34
	23		Took up a rear guard action retiring thro' PERONNE & CLERY & tents taking	14/14
	23/4		up a position near HERBÉCOURT	15/14
	24		Battn. retired across French line DOMPIERRE - FRISE & that night occupied a line in front of line HERBECOURT - FRISE retired at 1AM to B__ CAPPY	
	25/6		Battn. arrived at BOIS OLIMPI near CAPPY	17/3/4
	26		occupied a line S of CAPPY & having fought a Rear guard action retired on the PROYART - FRAMERVILLE LINE	18/14
	26/7		Retiring thro' PROYART - FRAMERVILLE LINE	1/1/4
	27		Battn. moved to MORCOURT & received Ridge between MORCOURT & PROYART namely Wanko?? + was ordered to retire on a __ some 500y of A were with orders to defend the Ridge PROYART + would any cost but were later when ordered on to MORCOURT and with orders to hold up Enemy until machine gun R.E.	18/11/4
	28		tooks up a position S.E. of HARLECAVE where heavily attacked Battn retired thro' HARLECAVE & took one posn. on 3rd R.I.R.	14/4
	28/9		Battn moved to line N.F. DEMUIN on line AUBERCOURT MANOR CAVE	14/4

Army Form C. 2118.

WAR DIARY
or
INTELLIGENCE SUMMARY.
(Erase heading not required.)

Instructions regarding War Diaries and Intelligence Summaries are contained in F. S. Regs., Part II. and the Staff Manual respectively. Title pages will be prepared in manuscript.

Place	Date 1918	Hour	Summary of Events and Information	Remarks and references to Appendices
	Mch 30		Battn moved to a wood N.W. of last position & occupied a line N of HANGARD. During the day the Battn was involved in checking enemy attacks held the line until relieved on the morning of 31st at 6 a.m. when it moved to LONGUEAU & marched thence to BOUZELLES.	N.A.
	30/1		Casualties for the month	N.A.
			killed wounded missing	
			Off. 1 Off. 4 = 10	
			OR. 47 OR 164 OR 105 = 316	
			Killed Lt. A.W.B. DAHNE 30.3.18 T/Capt. G.S.D. HILLIER 30.3.18	
			Wounded T/Capt. H. JONES M.C. 23.3.18 7/Lt H.B. HARVEY 30.3.18	N.A.
			" D.F. MOZLEY 30.3.18 7/Lt B.B. CALCUTT 30.3.18	
			" H.L.D. GILL M.C. date unknown 7/Lt F.C. BRIGHT 23.3.18	
			7/Lt W.L. TAYLOR 30.3.18	
			7/Lt R.H. ANDERSON 28.3.18	

R.A. Harman Major
1.4.18

for O.C. 13th Yorkshires

39th Division.

Composite Brigade

Pioneers 39th Div.

Formed part of No. 2 Composite Battalion 11.4.18.

1/13th BATTALION

GLOUCESTERSHIRE REGIMENT

APRIL 1918.

14 R/31 13 Gloucester Army Form C. 2118.

Ref Map 1/100000 AMIENS Sheet 17
DIEPPE Sheet 16

WAR DIARY
or
INTELLIGENCE SUMMARY
(Erase heading not required.)

VI 26
25N
7 sheets

Place	Date	Hour	Summary of Events and Information	Remarks and references to Appendices
	April 1918			
	2nd		Bn marched from BOVELLES to FRESNOY AU VAL & billetted for night	
	3rd		Bn marched to LINCHEUX & billetted for night	
	6th		Bn marched to FRESNEVILLE and billetted. Refitting commenced	
	6th		Bn marched to NESTLE LE HOPITAL & billetted for night	
	7th		Bn marched to MONCHAUX & billetted for night	
	8th		Bn marched to FRIACOURT & billetted	
	9th		Bn entrained at WOINCOURT for ST OMER	
	10th		Bn arrived ST OMER & billetted at ST MARTIN-AU-LAERT. About 10 km.	
			Message received that 13th Gloucesters would furnish 3 Coys. Also Each 150 strong with 3 officers to make up 13th Bn SUSSEX REGT. No 2 Coy of 13th Bn of 39th Div Comp's Brigade & at the same time furnish 9 officers for No 1 Comp'si Bn of same Brigade. No 2 Bn to entrain at ST OMER at 7AM 11-4-18. Bn Headquarters (13th Gloucesters) to form a cadre. Bn for training American troops belonging to 17th Div A.E.F. Comp'si Bn retained distinction unknown	
	11th 12th		13th GLOS headquarters moved to ZUDROVE	

WAR DIARY or **INTELLIGENCE SUMMARY.** Ref Sheet 1/40000 BELGIUM & FRANCE 28

Army Form C. 2118.

Place	Date	Hour	Summary of Events and Information	Remarks and references to Appendices
	1915 April 11		No 2 Company marched from VLAMERTINGHE, where they had bivouaced,	
			to ONTAWA CAMP	
	12		No 2 Coy marched to MAIDA CAMP	
	13		" " RIDGE WOOD heavily shelled several casualties.	See remarks
	16		No 2 Bn was handed over to 67th Bde 9th Division & marched to ROSSIGNOL Wood of May Gen	Cruez 9th Div
			& later moven forward to line VANDAMME FM. LAAGHE.FM. STORE.FM.	
			In evening 13th Bn in counter attack to recapture MEDELSTEDE.FM. and	attached.
WYTSCHAETE Wood				
	21		No 2 Bn rejoined original 39th Div comprising Bde & moved to DOMINION CAMP	
			9.2.b but were again put at disposal of 67th Bde 9th Division	
	24-25		No 2 Bn relieved 16 MANCHESTER REGT later, other troops having been pushed	
			back, No 2 Bn formed a defensive flank to SHELLY FARM to conform,	
			later it was ordered to hold the line BUS HOUSE (exclusive) – THE BLUFF (inclusive)	
	26		At 5.A.M. Enemy were wearing officials No 2 Bn but report failed to reach	
			Brigade Hq Qrs & S.O.S. owing to fog, down not seen by artillery – Enemy,	
			penetrated into our lines – reached the STOLZ BANK and attacked the BLUFF	

Army Form C. 2118.

WAR DIARY
or
INTELLIGENCE SUMMARY.
(Erase heading not required.)

Place	Date	Hour	Summary of Events and Information	Remarks and references to Appendices
	1918 April		Very few officers & men escaped and the survivors withdrew on Neuray of the CANAL to 110 Inf Bde line a short front W of the BLUFF held by Lt R.F. HALL with 1 Platoon of 13th GLOSTERS held our from 7.30AM to 5PM when surrounded by the enemy during the whole time; at 8 pm they fought their way out to our line the officer & 17 O.R. washing safely. Remainder of No 2 Company he were Annd generation with No 4 Company 18n of 39th Div Composite Bde	
	MAY 5th		[struck through] 39th Division's Survivors returned to our march by [illegible] reporting headquarters 13th GLOUCESTERS at REMINGHEM where that unit has engaged training American troops of 17th Div during training. Casualties for month: Killed: Off — , O.R. 3 Wounded: Off 1, O.R. 79 Missing: Off 5, O.R. 201 Killed Lt W.H. HOMER 26-4-18 Wounded Lt CDE DEWE 16-4-18 E.G. RICHARDS 25-4-18 R. HENDERSON BLAND 26-4-18 2/Lt A. TAPLIN 26-4-18 Missing: Major H. R. HOLLMAN 26-4-18 Capt. F.E.A. BERGER-WASLER " " " G.M. HELE " " " F.B. WHITTALL " " 2/Lt A.C. BAKER " " " L.C. FARR " " " J.S. PAWGEY " " " D.D. HERRING " " " F.S. SMITH " " " — HAGUE " "	

WAR DIARY
INTELLIGENCE SUMMARY

Army Form C. 2118.

Place	Date	Hour	Summary of Events and Information	Remarks and references to Appendices
	1918 April 30		Officers reported from England Capt H.J. HILLIER M.C. 22-4-18 Lt. F.B. WHITTALL 22-4-18 Posted to 13th Gloucesters & joined the Capt. G.G. ELLINGTON DSO 13-4-18 on date opposite - their names and 2nd Lt J DENHAM DCM 14-4-18 reported to 14th Gloucestershire Reg.t. J.N. HOOPER 17-4-18 18/4/18 - Approval was given to retain Capt C.G. ELLINGTON DSO with 13th GLOUCESTER Training Staff for A.E.F. Authority AG 2158/1837 (0) AWARDS. No 19393 L.Cpl LONERGAN V.J. Military Medal.	

A.M.Moulton Lt. Col.
O.C. 13th Gloucesters
9/5/18

Appendix

SPECIAL ORDER OF THE DAY

by

MAJOR GENERAL C. A. BLACKLOCK, C.M.G., D.S.O.,

Commanding 39th DIVISION.

----

1. The following letter has been received from the Major-General Commanding 9th DIVISION, with which Nos. 2 and 3 COMPOSITE BATTALIONS of the 39th DIVISION have recently been serving:-

> "I wish to express to you my appreciation of the fine fighting spirit shown by the 2nd and 3rd COMPOSITE BATTALIONS of the 39th DIVISION whilst fighting with the 9th DIVISION.
> In the counter attack on WYTSCHAETE on April 17th, these Battalions attacked alongside battalions of 9th and 21st DIVISIONS; the 3rd BATTALION penetrating into WYTSCHAETE; and the 2nd BATTALION advancing our line materially, in the direction of BOIS DE WYTSCHAETE in spite of enfilade fire from SPANBROEKMOLEN.
> Will you please also express to your Battalion Commanders my regret at not being able to see them personally before they left my command."

2. The Major-General Commanding wishes to congratulate the 13th ROYAL SUSSEX Regt., the 16th NOTTS & DERBY REGT., the 17th K.R.R.CORPS and the 16th RIFLE BRIGADE, and the 13th BN. GLOUCESTERSHIRE REGT., on the gallant way in which they have maintained the reputation of their regiments, and of their Division.

3. This order will be read aloud to all troops of the Division on parade on the first suitable occasion, under arrangements to be made by O.C. Units.

(Sd.) F. W. GOSSET, Lieut-Colonel
General Staff, 39th Div.

25th April, 1918.

Letter from SIR A. J. GODLEY, K.C.B., K.C.M.G., Commanding XXII Corps to MAJ.-GEN. C. A. BLACKLOCK, C.M.G., D.S.O., Cmdg. 39th DIVISION:-

            Headquarters,
             XXII Corps.
             4th May, 1918.

Dear Blacklock,

  On the departure of the COMPOSITE BRIGADE of your DIVISION from my CORPS, I write to let you know that it has done most excellent service during the time that it has been with us, both on the WYTSCHAETE RIDGE, and afterwards on the VIERSTRAAT LINE it did very fine work, and I should be glad if you would convey to GEN. HUBBACK and all ranks of his command my thanks and appreciation of their services.

      Yours sincerely,

       Sd. ALEX. GODLEY.

Letter from B.G.C. 39th COMPOSITE BRIGADE to all Units:-

            Headquarters,
             118 Inf. Bde.
             6. 5. 18.

  As the 39th DIVISION COMPOSITE BRIGADE has now ceased to exist, I desire to express my sincere thanks to all ranks for the splendid manner in which they have responded to the very severe calls made upon them.

  The gallantry and devotion to duty shown in the operations around WYTSCHAETE & VOORMEZEELE are beyond all praise, and all ranks have worthily maintained the high traditions of the 39th DIVISION.

  I much regret that I have no longer the honour of commanding officers and men who have shown such a fine fighting spirit.

       Sd. A. B. HUBBACK, Brig.-Gen.
        Cmdg. 118th Infy. Brigade.

Copy.

30.4.18.

Dear Boulton,

I thought you and the Regiment would like to know the following, which occurs in a private letter I have received from Marr, and shown to the G.O.C:-

"A Gloucester Officer, named HALL, with No.2. Bn. put up a remarkably fine show on the 26th. He was surrounded by the Bosche (and his platoon) near the BLUFF about 7.30 a.m., and maintained his position until 8 p.m., when he fought his way through, and rejoined the remnants of No.2. Bn. with 17 men. The Gloucesters have fought magnificently throughout."

May I offer you and the Regiment my heartiest congratulations?

A general message has also been received by the Composite Brigade, which is being issued as a "Special Order of the Day" by the G.O's.C. instructions.

Yours,

(Sd.) F. W. GOSSET.

R/38 13th Bn
Army Form C. 2118.

WAR DIARY
INTELLIGENCE SUMMARY
(Erase heading not required.)

Ref maps HAZEBROUCK 5A
CALAIS Sheet 13
Vol. 27

Place	Date	Hour	Summary of Events and Information	Remarks and references to Appendices
	1918 MAY 5-6		Survivors of 13th Gloucesters by O.R. from No 2 Composite Bn. & 8 Officers from No 1 Composite Bn. rejoined their unit at ROMARIN 39th Div. Composite Bde being disbanded. From these survivors the Cadre bn was constituted also a demobilization Platoon was selected (entitlia). Demobilization platoon eventually disallowed & demobilization sections only permitted of officers NCOs men being sent to RIFLES for clothing & other small demobilization, section (39th div Demobilization in turning Cadres bn (surviving) returned to 12th (Gloucesters) went to LA MOTRIRE from where surviving men & Lieutenant over to above establishment. Authorised for a running Cadre bn. up. On CABLES the last draft being dispatched on 16/5/18 completing the disbandment on a fighting unit. The battalion all ranks was now known as for training cadres.	
	"		Moved to SUNGHEN to organize area for training cadres	
	"		BELLE	

26 N
3 May

WAR DIARY
or
INTELLIGENCE SUMMARY.

Army Form C. 2118.

Place	Date	Hour	Summary of Events and Information	Remarks and references to Appendices
			Officers reported to other Units on dates opposite their names Lt R V BIRCH to 1/4th Glos 23/3/18	
			2Lt R G LEE " 28/3/18	
			Lt O P QUINTON " "	
			2Lt R H WEST " "	
			2Lt R M ANDERSON 2/5th Glos "	
			2Lt G W FARRINGTON 12/6th Glos 4/5/18	
			2Lt REF MAA 9/5/18	
			Evacuated to England Sick	
			HODGES + EDWARDS	
			Mentioned in Sir Douglas Haig's despatch 7/4/18	
			Capt G M BELL	
			Lt M SMITH	
			No 2783 RSM C PRIORY	
			Awarded DCM 38703 Pte W EDWARDS	
			267425 Sergt F JOYNER	
			7869 L/Cpl F PREECE		MAB

WAR DIARY
or
INTELLIGENCE SUMMARY.
(Erase heading not required.)

Army Form C. 2118.

Place	Date	Hour	Summary of Events and Information	Remarks and references to Appendices
AWARDS M.M.			No 15012 Cpl G.E. POWELL	
			19276 L.Cpl S.W. HAYNES	
			15076 Pte L.G. NICHOLSON	
			A.J. Mullin? Lt Col	
			O.C. 13th Gloucesters	

Secret Confidential

WAR DIARY or INTELLIGENCE SUMMARY.
Army Form C. 2118.

13th Glous Regt 39

Vol 28

Place	Date	Hour	Summary of Events and Information	Remarks and references to Appendices
	1915 June		13th GLOS MOVED to BLEMBOM. Ref. Maps PARIS 12, HAZEBROUCK S-7 Regt. H.Q. not prepared moved in support of sec Ts. 115th Engineer Regt. 30th Div. A.E.F.	111
	June 15		Regt. H.Q. and one Coy American Engineers arrived	111
	June 16		Remainder of 115th Engineer Regt arrived. PIETZBON into Training commenced	111
	May 28		13th GLOS accompanying 105th Eng Regt in an advisory capacity arrived BIRMINGHAM	11?
	May 22		Were continued to BAGUES	11?
	May 23		Were continued to CASSEL area where 105th Engineer Regt. in Trench Training	
			and also with 2d MUNIZIELE. East Artillerie	11?

Casualties - Nil Adm. UR nil

Officers 1st Bn Glos Reg: (AG/4270(a) 7-6-18)

Cpl H.H. VOWLES
Lt M. SMITH
Lt H.G. REECE
Lt F.I. LOVELL
2/Lt W.D. BELL
2/Lt F.W. WILKINSON
2/Lt S.J.V. ROACH
2/Lt A.C. HOLBOROW

Army Form C. 2118.

WAR DIARY
or
INTELLIGENCE SUMMARY.
(Erase heading not required.)

Adv. Maps HAZEBROUCK 5A } 1/40,000
CALAIS 13 }

WO 95/29

Place	Date	Hour	Summary of Events and Information	Remarks and references to Appendices
	1918			
	July 10		10th Engineer Regt accompanied by Hq & 2nd Bn Hq remainder of 13th Platoon moved to forward	
			area. Remainder of 13th Platoon moved to WATTEN	
	July 11		Bn moved from WATTEN to LUMBRES Hq and 2 Sqns Hq remainder opened to warriors	
	July 27		Bn moved from LUMBRES to JEUSE	
			Casualties:—	
			Off. Ord. 1 Rn. Ord.	

Ghent Sept 7th 1918
Lt. Col.
O.C. 13th (FOREST OF DEAN) BAT.
THE GLOUCESTERSHIRE REGIMENT

CONFIDENTIAL

WAR DIARY

OF

13th GLOUCESTERS

FROM :- Aug 1st 1918
TO :- " 31st "

VOL N°

Army Form C. 2118.

WAR DIARY
or
INTELLIGENCE SUMMARY.
(Erase heading not required.)

Place: Rimy
Hazebrouck 5ᴬ
Calais 15
Dieppe 16

Date	Hour	Summary of Events and Information	Remarks and references to Appendices
1918			
Aug 15		Bn left YEUSE by march route and entrained at NORDHERQUE at 6 pm	[init]
Aug 16		Arrived at ABANCOURT 9 am	[init]
Aug 29		Moved from ABANCOURT to encampment at HAUDRICOURT	[init]
Aug 31		Bn transferred from 39th Division to 66th Division	[init]
		Casualties	
		1 offr. and 1 O.R. wtd	

[signature]
OC 13 Cheshire

A6945 Wt W11422/M1160 350,000 12/16 D.D. & L. Forms/C/2118/14.

WAR DIARY
INTELLIGENCE SUMMARY

Army Form C.2118.

Reb Group
DIEPPE 16 1/00,000   Vol 31

Place	Date	Hour	Summary of Events and Information	Remarks and references to Appendices
	1918 Sept		Preparing Court at HAUDRICOURT for reception of "Evidoria" reinforcements	
	Sept 16		first reinforcements draft to them sails arrived and Administration begun	
			Arrivals	
			OR Nil ORs Nil	
			Attached Capt Tetley for att 125 Platoon	

30N
2 sheet

WAR DIARY
INTELLIGENCE SUMMARY

Army Form C. 2118.

REF MAP DIEPPE 1/100,000

Place	Date	Hour	Summary of Events and Information	Remarks and references to Appendices
	1919			
	Oct.		Inconnu Material Reinforcements in Camp at HAUDRICOURT	
	21/24		First draft of 143 O.Rs. proceeded to Base on reinforcements.	
			Casualties	
			Off. Nil O.Rs. 1 died in hospital	

Martin Cpt RE
for O.C.
13th Coy (L of C Troops) R.E.

C O N F I D E N T I A L.

W A R   D I A R Y

O F

13th. Battalion GLOUCESTERSHIRE REGIMENT

From :-, 1st. Novr. 1918.   To :- 30th. Novr. 1918.

Army Form C. 2118

WAR DIARY
or
INTELLIGENCE SUMMARY
(Erase heading not required.)

REF MAP DIEPPE 16/100,000

Instructions regarding War Diaries and Intelligence Summaries are contained in F.S. Regs., Part II. and the Staff Manual respectively. Title Pages will be prepared in manuscript.

Place	Date	Hour	Summary of Events and Information	Remarks and references to Appendices
	Nov 1918 11th		Administering "Malaria reinforcements at HAVORICOURT. Armistice signed. Casualties:- Offrs nil O.R. nil Promotions:- T/Major W.M. de PAULA M.C. to Lt A/Col. whilst Commanding Bn. 15 July 1918 (Supp London Gazette 29 Oct 1918)	Not 3 (Own)

W.M. de Paula Lt Col
O.C. 13 Battalion

32N
2 sheet

WAR DIARY
or
INTELLIGENCE SUMMARY

Army Form C. 2118

REF MAPS
DIEPPE 1/3 Gloucester [Regt?]

Place	Date 1915	Hour	Summary of Events and Information	Remarks and references to Appendices
HAVRE/[ROUEN?]	Sep 4		Under orders from 197 2nd Bde landed over Material Personnel (365 O.Rs) 10% Bn. Lincoln Regt.- Entrained at AUMALE for HAVRE under orders of 116 Inf Bde	
Dieppe			Commenced disembarkation of P. & D men and Minors at No 1 Camp Section B - ,, -	
		1.10		
			Casualties:- Off nil. O.R. nil. Nurses, [?]	
			Minors:- Capt G.M. HELE Capt B.J. LAMPLUGH Capt QM S.T. ROWLINSON C.S.M. H. KILBY	

[signature] O.C.
13th [?] BEAM BATT. GLOSTER REGT.

39. 4/3 × PYB 13 Gloucester Vol 35

Army Form C. 2118.

WAR DIARY
INTELLIGENCE SUMMARY
(Erase heading not required.)

Place	Date 1919	Hour	Summary of Events and Information	Remarks and references to Appendices
LE HAVRE	Jan 1/31		Cadre employed at No 1 Despatching Camp in dismantling.	
			Casualties — Off. Nil O.R. Nil	
			Rejoined: Lt J.H. Marshall struck off from A.Q. 2-1-19	
			Lt W.H.G. Paul Gidddus 3-1-19	
			Lt H.R. Lowe MC Posted from 2/5 Glosters 6-1-19	
			To England dismantling:—	
			Capt I.C. Proctor MC 26-1-19	
			Capt H.D. Hillier MC 29-1-19	
			Lt W.A.G. Park - Gidddms - 29-1-19	

66 JN 19? BK 32-5

[signature] Lt. Col
O.C. 13 Glosters

Army Form C. 2118A

WAR DIARY
INTELLIGENCE SUMMARY

(Erase heading not required.)

13 Gloucester

Place	Date 1919	Hour	Summary of Events and Information	Remarks and references to Appendices
LE HAVRE	Feb 1/28		Ladies employed at No 1 Despatching Camp on demobilization	BM
			Casualties Officers 4. ORs Nil.	
			Rejoined from leave to U.K:—	
			Capt. B.J. LAMPLUGH. 5.2.19	
			Lieut. A.J. RADLEY 8.2.19	
			" P.E. GARDINER 17.2.19	
			To ENGLAND demobilized:—	
			Lieut Col. W.M. de PAULA. M.C. 27.2.19	
			Capt. C.G. ELKINGTON. D.S.O 3.2.19	
			To ENGLAND Sick:—	
			Lieut H.R. LOWE. M.C. 21.2.19	
			Strength & establishment of this Unit 14/9/18 on being returned in U.K. for demobilization.	
			Lieut. E.C. HALTON.	
			AUTH. AG No AG/2153/901B (O) 2-2-19	
			DAG. CR No 12650/465/A 3-2-19	
			B Lamplugh Capt.	
			For 13th Gloucestershire Regt.	

Army Form C. 2118.

WAR DIARY
or
INTELLIGENCE SUMMARY.

13 Gloucester
WO 37

(Erase heading not required.)

Instructions regarding War Diaries and Intelligence Summaries are contained in F. S. Regs., Part II. and the Staff Manual respectively. Title pages will be prepared in manuscript.

Place	Date	Hour	Summary of Events and Information	Remarks and references to Appendices
LE HAVRE	1919 March 1/31		Codies employed at No 1 Despatching Camp on demobilization	
	26		Received the following from 116th Infantry Brigade	
			Casualties Officers Nil ORs 4. (Demobilized)	

B.F.Kavanaugh
Capt.
O C 13th Gloucestershire Regt

Army Form C. 2118.

13 Gloucester

WAR DIARY
or
INTELLIGENCE SUMMARY.
(Erase heading not required.)

Instructions regarding War Diaries and Intelligence Summaries are contained in F. S. Regs., Part II. and the Staff Manual respectively. Title pages will be prepared in manuscript.

87N Issue

Place	Date	Hour	Summary of Events and Information	Remarks and references to Appendices
LE HAVRE	April 1919 1/30		Cadre employed at No 1 Despatching Camp to demobilization.	199
	15		Returned to concentration of the Cadre in the presence of the G.O.C. Base Division.	
	25		Under orders received from 16th Infantry Bde H.Qrs duties in connection with demobilization above handed over to the 18th Bn the Middlesex Regiment.	
			Casualties	
			Officers 1 ORs Nil	
			Capt. B. J. LAMPLUGH to Hospital 23.4.19	

P. J. Philpins
Lieut.
O.C. 13th Gloucester

WAR DIARY or INTELLIGENCE SUMMARY.

Army Form C. 2118.

13 Gloucesters

Place	Date 1919	Hour	Summary of Events and Information	Remarks and references to Appendices
LE HAVRE	May 1/31			
	2		Presentation of the King's Colours by Maj. Gen. H.C.C. UNIACKE, CB, CMG.	
	3		Cadre transferred from administration of 116 Inf. Brigade to 197 Inf. Brigade	
	13		Reporter from Hospital — Capt. B. J. LAMPLUGH.	
			Casualties	
			Officers NIL ORs 8 (demobilized)	

P. Gardner
Capt & O/C
1st Capt